COUGAR

Ghost of the Rockies

Karen McCall and Jim Dutcher

Foreword by Wallace Stegner
Introduction by Maurice Hornocker

SIERRA CLUB BOOKS
San Francisco

Library of Congress Cataloging in Publication Data

Dutcher, Jim, 1943–
    Cougar : ghost of the Rockies / by Jim Dutcher and Karen McCall.
    p. cm.
    Includes index.
    ISBN 0-87156-564-1
    1. Pumas. I. McCall, Karen, 1950– . II. Title.
QL737.C23D87   1992
599.74′428—dc20   92-3691
                                CIP

Additional photographs provided by:
Johann Guschelbauer (pages 21, 98, and 141), Jake Provonsha (pages 51, 106, 109, 110, and 130), Don MacCarter (page 46), and Dennis Kane (page 130)

Production by Janet Vail

Book design and jacket design by Mark Ong

Printed in Hong Kong by South Sea International Press, Ltd.

Contents

Memo to the Mountain Lion

Once, in every corner of this continent, your passing could prickle the stillness and bring every living thing to the alert. But even then you were more felt than seen. You were an imminence, a presence, a crying in the night, pug tracks in the dust of a trail. Solitary and shy, you lived beyond, always beyond. Your comings and goings defined the boundaries of the unpeopled. If seen at all, you were only a tawny glimpse flowing toward disappearance among the trees or along the ridges and ledges of your wilderness.

But hunters, with their dogs and guns, knew how to find you. Folklore made you dangerous, your occasional killing of a calf put a price on your head. Never mind that you preferred deer, that your killings of livestock were trivial by comparison with those by our own dogs. You were wild, and thus an enemy; you were rare, and elusive, and elegant, and thus a trophy to be prized. Under many names, as panther, catamount, puma, cougar, mountain lion, you were hunted to death through all the East and Midwest. The last catamount in Vermont was shot more than a hundred years ago. You persist in the Everglades only because a National Park official quietly released a pair of you to restore the life-balance of that fecund swamp.

In the mountain and plateau West a remnant population of you persists, in the pockets of wild country off the edges of settlement and too rough for off-road vehicles. If you kill a calf or a sheep, the permit hunters still exact a more-than-eye-for-an-eye vengeance, but in California, at least, a moratorium on ordinary hunting has let your numbers stabilize. The Fish and Game people say there are 2,400 of you in California. A better guess is 1,000. But a remnant. There is a chance you may survive.

You had better. If we lift the moratorium that has helped to save you, we are insane. Visiting Africa, twentieth-century Americans are struck by how poor we have become, how poor we have made ourselves, how much pleasure and instruction we have deprived ourselves of, by our furious destruction of other species.

Controls we may need, what is called game-management we may need, for we have engrossed the earth and must now play God to the other species. But deliberate war on any species, especially species of such evolved beauty and precise function, diminishes, endangers, and brutalizes us. If we cannot live in harmony with other forms of life, if we cannot control our hostility toward the earth and its creatures, how shall we ever learn to control our hostility toward each other?

Wallace Stegner
Los Altos Hills, California

Introduction

The mountain lion is a remarkable animal. It can live in deserts or rain forests, mountains or plains. It can live on animals the size of hares or the size of elk. It once lived in every corner of our forty-eight contiguous United States and ranged from central British Columbia to the tip of South America—the widest distribution of any animal in the Western Hemisphere.

Persecuted unmercifully for over two hundred years in North America, the lion hung on in the mountains and the canyons of the West. Now, because of new information and a changed attitude toward all wildlife, the lion is offered some protection. It has come back in numbers in the West and has again assumed its natural position in the ecologic scheme of things—at the absolute apex of the food chain. The mountain lion exerts an influence over everything below it, an influence that has evolved over millions of years.

I have studied the mountain lion for almost twenty-five years. My associates and I have intensively researched populations of lions from Montana to New Mexico, from Idaho to Wyoming, with Yellowstone in between. We have uncovered the secrets of this "cat of one color," and this new knowledge has formed the basis for programs aimed at conserving the lion.

As a scientist, I must view my subject in an objective, "scientific" manner. But once in a while it is appropriate to step back and view natural phenomena through an artistic aperture. There are times when the sheer beauty of nature, when the whole patchwork and its individual pieces, should be appreciated for the miracle it truly is.

This is what this book does. Jim Dutcher and Karen McCall are artists unencumbered by scientific objectivity. This book is their personal look at a very special piece of nature's patchwork through their own subjective viewfinder. Karen's words recount their experiences with a mountain lion reared in captivity, and Jim's photographs document the unique story visually. Their emotions as artists and human beings show through. Their sensitivity to their subject almost, but not quite, overshadows their craft. The result is a work that gives us insight and appreciation for the beauty and grace of an animal that is truly, in Wallace Stegner's words, "of evolved beauty and precise function."

Maurice Hornocker, Director
Hornocker Wildlife Research Institute

Acknowledgments

In the spring of 1988, Jim Dutcher invited me to join the film crew of his mountain lion project. My role as researcher evolved into that of scribe for Jim's intimate narrative—a unique journey with mountain lion and western landscape. My words, nurtured by Jim's recollection, and his exquisite photographs collaborate to tell a story. Stories open doors to wildness.

As always, in long-term projects, there are many participants, whose creativity and persistence are essential: Dennis Kane, David O'Dell, and Debbie Rothberg in Washington, D.C.; Sharon Negri and the Mountain Lion Foundation shared their research and passion for a magnificent cat; Barb Heller and Kerry Murphy shared stories of unusual cougar experiences in the wild.

Patty and Jake Provonsha provided us with wit, laughter, and logic at our camp in the White Clouds. This project would not have been possible without Brent Snyder and Kathy Rogerson's responsible caretaking of the cougars in our absence. A special thanks to Garrick Dutcher. Bob Pearson, Ridley Pearson, Karen Oswalt, Cheryl Welch, Rich Bray, and Teresa Heinz all contributed to our perception of what this book could be.

And to Jan Roddy, we are grateful for her perseverance and the experiences we share in wild places.

Karen McCall

For wildness

1

The Ghost

A horizontal shaft of saffron light haloes a female mountain lion as she silently, sinuously descends from a high rock precipice. She is alert, restless, and yet she moves with an elegant mystique gifted only to felines. As her long tail oscillates from side to side its sepia-colored tip cuts a swath through the afternoon's dusting of spring snow.

Catapulting off her athletic hind legs so superbly adapted for the diversity of her habitat's rugged topography, the female springs over an immense, fallen Douglas fir. Gliding fully outstretched, forepaws to balancing tail tip, she measures eight and a half feet. Her landing, within an unforgiving entanglement of debris from an avalanche of several winters past, is flawlessly adroit — estimation and experience synchronized for precision. A striped chipmunk is startled and bolts away. Barely giving it a glance the lion travels on. She has other things on her mind. Her descent is deliberate.

The lion I see in my mind's eye is not quite three years old. She left her mother's protection seventeen months ago and, until recently, she has been a solitary wanderer in search of her own territory. Although she is young, she weighs one hundred and ten pounds, surpassing the weight of her own mother. As the daylight dims, her

Aglow with low evening light, a mountain lion scans her domain.

coat loses its golden hue. It is now ashen, dusky like the twilight. Her most distinguishable markings are the black backs of her slightly pointed ears and the "butterfly" formation of white and black around her mouth.

Closer to the bottom of the slope, travelling between the intermingling zones of Douglas fir and ponderosa pine, she approaches the canyon drainage. She avoids walking in a straight path and zigzags through a dense cover of spiny underbrush. Lurking in the shadows, a nebulous creature in the half-light.

Taking a step, she recoils, lifts her forepaw, and shakes it vigorously. A large thorn has pierced the sensitive pad and she stops to rid herself of its stinging pain. Her paws, at three and a half inches wide, are wider than they are long by a half an inch. Scientists know that the paws, the toes, and the tip of the nose on the mountain lion are acutely sensitive. It is assumed that the vibrissae, the stiff, white whiskers growing from the black patches near the mouth and nostrils, serve as organs of touch, antennae to define passable spaces. The removal of these hairs could temporarily disable the animal until new whiskers grow.

The day's light fades further. A raven flies from the pinnacle of a ponderosa and interrupts the evening silence with a grating *c-r-r-r-u-u-k, c-r-r-r-u-u-k*. The lion moves alongside a massive boulder, sliding her flank along its mottled wall of granite. She stops to rub her ears and the length of her body luxuriously against the rock's jagged extrusions. After her massage, she walks on. Moments later, she ascends a small boulder and scans the meadow on the far side of the creek. She looks for movement. In the twilight, close to the forest's edge, a herd of elk, seven cows and three calves, paw the ground, grazing on the scant leaves and grasses revealed by the melting winter snowpack. The lion, now a hunter, sharpens her focus. Her extraordinary vision is unhampered by the crepuscular hour, for she has a metallic, mirrorlike lustre of crystals called the tapetum behind the retina that reflects almost invisible light and amplifies her visual acuity.

Quickly changing weather and light in Idaho's White Cloud Mountains provide a mysterious, dreamlike backdrop for the film project's cougar enclosure and camp.

Silent and alert, the cougar stalks without distraction.

With fixed gaze and ears pricked forward she draws nearer in a silent, stealthy stalk. A coyote scampers off, relinquishing his right to any smaller prey in the lion's territory. The lion edges forward. Raising her head, a cow elk senses something amiss, but, seeing and scenting nothing, she returns to feeding. A nine-month-old calf, however, lingers behind and in moments is separated from its mother.

The lion creeps closer. Because her energy is limited by lung capacity to brief, forty-mile-an-hour sprints, she must get to within striking range without startling her prey. She stalks still closer in a slinking, vigilant crouch hidden behind boulders and camouflaged by the ground cover. Intuiting the perfect moment, an instant of carelessness by her victim, she leaps, her powerful hind legs launching her through the air like a horizontal bolt of lightning.

She lands and springs again, muscles taut, forelegs reaching in an unbelievable extension for the neck of the elk. She strikes the calf with a locomotive force that instantly knocks it to the ground. Grasping the head in her paws with claws released, one dewclaw spearing the hide, she twists the elk's neck. It breaks with a snap.

▾ ▾ ▾

The lion is *Felis concolor*. It is a member of the family *Felidae*, the genus *Felis*, and the subgenus *Puma*. *Felis concolor* is Latin for "the cat of all one color." Although its kittens are born with the vestigial spots of its ancestral species, these markings most often vanish by six months when the lion's coat assumes a blended coloration described as ashen, gray, tawny, golden, apricot, cinnamon, silver, or chestnut. The individual hairs are tipped with sepia or slate gray tones that alter the color of the coat in changing light. Lighter colored, even white fur covers the underside of the cougar where the hair is the longest. Sightings of black cougars are reported in North America, but are questioned by most biologists as either folkloric throw-backs to the early settlers' fearful image of the cougar as a black panther, or are

Along with deer and bighorn sheep, the elk or "Wapiti" is a primary food source for the mountain lion.

The mountain valleys of Idaho burst with color from spring through summer as wildflowers eke out a high desert existence. Here lupine and sego lillies dapple the landscape.

Alert to all predators, the snowshoe hare usually spends the daytime in cover and feeds at night in the open. Large, long-furred feet ease travel on heavy snow.

attributed to a genetic deviation causing melanism. There are no records of albino cougars, but there is archeological evidence that Aztec ritual used the sharpened bones of the white puma to ward off death from ailing tribal members.

The subgenus classification *Puma* derives from a name first used by the Incas of Peru and is the appellation most universally used for this cat. However, myriad names have evolved from the species' wide geographic distribution, various colors, and enigmatic behavior.

In North America the common name "cougar" is a corruption of the native Brazilian *cuguacuarana*. In 1776 the French naturalist Buffon applied his version, *le couguar,* to a subspecies in Pennsylvania, Georgia, and the Carolinas. When Christopher Columbus landed off Honduras in 1502, he saw a large cat that resembled the African lioness. He spoke of it as *leon.*

Europeans settling on the Atlantic seaboard of North America were understandably frightened by this large feline they rarely saw. The names they gave it reflected their misconceptions about the cat's ferocity and elusiveness. Initially it was called a leopard because its young were found with spots. But because the spots disappeared, the settlers claimed it was a panther—a vicious cat that dragged babies from their cribs at night. "Painter," a colloquialism evolving from panther, became common in New England. Tiger, screamer, devil cat, Indian devil, catamount, and ghost cat were all popular names in early American lore. It was not until the mountain men made their way west, trapping and hunting for the pelt trade, that the cougar received a more worthy name from the white man—the mountain lion.*

---

*For the sake of variety, puma, cougar, and mountain lion are used interchangeably throughout the book.

Native peoples selected names reflecting either a spiritual or pragmatic connection with the cougar. Survival being the primary focus, animals embodying qualities related to hunting were given the greatest significance and power. The bear was esteemed for its strength, the wolf for its endurance, the eagle for its vision. The mountain lion is prominent in tribal mythology for its cunning and stealth. To the Cherokees, the cougar was *Klandaghi,* the lord of the forest. To the Creeks it was *Katalgar,* greatest of wild hunters. Like the tribes of the eastern woods, the Zuni of the desert Southwest respected the cougar for its hunting prowess and called it "the father of game." The tribe followed the cougar and scavenged its kills. The meat constituted a substantial part of their diet.

There was a time when thirty subspecies of *Felis concolor* collectively held the widest distribution of any predator species in the Western Hemisphere. Because of its easy adaptability to almost any habitat and environmental conditions, the puma's historical disbursement covered one hundred degrees in latitude, from the northern extremities of British Columbia to the southern tip of Patagonia. Displaying amazing climatic and geographic diversity, the puma is known to live at elevations as high as 15,000 feet in the Andes, as well as in the tropical jungles of Costa Rica and the semiarid zones of the southwestern United States. Although the mountain lion was once pervasive, its international distribution is now sadly limited to the narrow mountainous corridor that stretches from Canada through Central America down into South America.

At one time, the lion roamed most of the United States from coastal New England to the Florida Everglades, across the plains and into the Rocky Mountains and the Sierra Nevada of California. Now, however, the cougar lives in eleven western states: Arizona, California, Colorado, Idaho, Montana, Nevada, New Mexico, Oregon, Utah, Washington, and Wyoming.

Grooming in typical feline fashion, a cougar gently licks her paw. The sandpaper tongue of the cougar is abrasive enough to lick flesh from the bones of prey.

Although cougars are not fond of water, they have been seen drifting down swift-flowing rivers and swimming along the coast of Vancouver from one island to another in search of deer.

Two remnant populations of the subspecies *Felis concolor coryi* (the Florida Panther) total fifty cougars living in the Florida Everglades. They are protected by the Endangered Species Act, yet they are still severely threatened by rapidly increasing human activity that jeopardizes their habitat. Biologists believe the two populations are pocketed, or isolated genetically. They have developed signs of inbreeding that may affect reproductive capabilities and the animal's resistance to disease and environmental fluctuations. Two-thirds of the panthers have been captured in an attempt to establish a breeding program between the separate bloodlines.

However successfully the captive breeding attempt may evolve, consider that the ultimate fate of the Florida Panther and the mountain lion will depend on sufficient protected wildlands and humankind's understanding that we are an integral part of the cougar's destiny.

Stark facial patterning on *Felis concolor,* the "cat of all one color," is the only remnant of its juvenile spots.

2

In Preparation

The spring rains had encouraged a rich, velvet-green veil to envelope the foothills of the surrounding mountain ranges. Spiky shoots of wild grasses surged their way through the moist soil and, on close view, scattered the ground with clustered spears of verdure. The ubiquitous sagebrush had lost its dry taupe hue and was now muted blue-green. May and June bring breath back to the Rocky Mountains, after months of winter stillness.

I had spent those long winter days in my Idaho cabin designing a strategy for making a film about the cougar. I studied stacks of information about the animal— scientific research, magazine articles, old *National Geographic* pieces, and individual accounts of cougar sightings. The most significant initial information I discovered was that the cougar is an elusive, secretive, and phantomlike animal that offers man only ephemeral glimpses. For the sake of survival it has learned to shun its only natural enemy by establishing territories far removed from the intrusion of humans. It also became clear from my reading and discussions with Dr. Maurice Hornocker that filming a cougar in the wild is impossible. (Dr. Hornocker is director of the Wildlife Research Institute, a foundation affiliated with the University of Idaho and the National Wildlife Federation. His pioneering research on the mountain lion has been the basis for all subsequent field studies.)

A wilderness recluse, the mountain lion must be assured sufficient habitat if it is to survive an ever-growing human population.

Having embraced naturalist Aldo Leopold's concept of wilderness as a natural laboratory because it is the "most perfect norm," Hornocker began his research in Idaho's Primitive Area, now the Frank Church River of No Return Wilderness. The 2.3-million-acre preserve in central Idaho is the largest contiguous tract of officially designated wilderness in the continental United States. Most of the landscape is heavily forested with ponderosa pine and Douglas fir and its protected status exempts its trees from the rapacious blades of the timber industry. This is roadless territory for the most part; all wheeled vehicles are excluded in favor of hiking boots and horses' hooves. Extensive trail systems access deep canyons that wall the rapid-filled courses of the South Fork and the Middle Fork of the Salmon River. The 425-mile Salmon drops seven thousand feet from its source in the upper Stanley Basin until it pours into the Snake River in Lewiston, Idaho. This roadless wilderness provides the necessary habitat for all wildlife that thrives away from contact with human populations.

Using radio-telemetry techniques developed by grizzly bear researchers John and Frank Craighead, Hornocker was able to monitor the seasonal movements of individual lions in a two-hundred-square-mile area of rugged terrain in the Big Creek drainage. Radio-collared cougars revealed heretofore unknown information about their social organization, spatial arrangements, territorial behavior, predation, family structure, and local population.

Hornocker's research on the cougar has helped alter America's traditional, apprehensive view of the cougar as an innately evil animal whose behavior was a deliberate act against man and nature. The first settlers in the East and then the pioneers moving into the "untame" and "uncivilized" West believed that they had a legitimate and moral right to kill the cougar before it killed them, their livestock, or the deer they hunted. Along with changing perceptions and a blossoming appreciation of wildlife in the 1960s, Hornocker's research helped erase some basic misconceptions about the cougar. He concluded that although mountain lions prey heavily on ungulates (deer and elk), their predation cannot impede a healthy population. Moreover, the lion regulates deer populations by dispersal and dampens the great fluctuations in numbers that occur with insufficient forage due to overgrazing. In essence, predation was determined to be beneficial in wilderness and semi-wilderness areas. Hornocker's research influenced legislation that changed the mountain lion's classification from "varmint" to "big game" animal. This reclassification effectively eliminated the killing of cougars for bounty and planted the seeds of respect for the cougar as a symbol of America's wild and free places.

On Hornocker's advice, I decided to locate a site where a large enclosure could be built. Although a wilderness setting would most closely resemble a natural situation, the restriction on motorized transportation eliminated this idea. I looked for some private or Forest Service land where I might gain permission to enclose a cougar for a year or more. Finally, a friend told me about a canyon on Forest Service land, blocked by a locked gate on a private ranch. The site was perfect. There was a variety of terrain, a very important element in my efforts to show the cougar's behavior in its natural habitat. A well-wooded young aspen grove, interspersed with twelve- to thirty-foot Douglas firs, grew next to a spring-fed stream that would provide drinking water year-round without freezing in winter or flooding with the heavy snowmelt. There were signs of beavers about: cut trees, a small pond, and a beaver-built dam. I hoped the still water would entice wild ducks. Dozens of ground squirrels and chipmunks and a few rabbits made their home here. Two enormous Douglas firs grew just below a hillside covered with granite crags and huge lichen-covered boulders.

To keep the location as much of a secret as possible from the local population, a

The original conservationist, the beaver creates a lush ecosystem—forage and water for deer, elk, and moose, cover for birdlife.

Beaver, badger, ground squirrel, porcupine, rabbit, and raccoon are secondary prey for the cougar. Competitors like the fox, coyote, lynx, and bobcat are killed by the cougar if found scavenging her cache.

fence company in Montana was contracted to build the enclosure. Previous experiences forewarned me about the hazards of publicity and excess attention drawn to projects about wildlife. I had spent fifteen years observing beavers at a mountain pond that served as the setting for my *National Geographic* film *A Rocky Mountain Beaver Pond*. The family of beavers had built an elaborate dam to create a pond in which their lodge was constructed. I filmed these animals nightly for years, and they became so accustomed to my presence that they would walk to within a few feet of my camera and busily go about their beaver ways, chomping on aspen or willow branches. Little by little, more people became aware of the beavers and the film project. One evening after the film was completed, I drove to the pond to visit the beavers and discovered that their den had been destroyed. Nothing was left but the charred and empty remains of a once thriving beaver colony. A hole had been dug through the living cavity and gasoline poured through the opening and set afire. There were no beavers in sight and the bank of the pond was strewn with shotgun shells. Vandalism of nature's creatures is incomprehensible to me and an overwhelming sadness stabbed my heart. I came to love the beavers I filmed. I knew one from another, I gave them names. They taught me their vital role in the ecosystem. I filmed them to help protect their species—and, in the process, I inadvertently put them at risk. As detached as I was biologically and culturally, I was linked by my emotions and intellect. The brutal death these animals suffered did not pass without terrible pain and a desperate attempt to protect their young—an effort, I think, that any human would make. Yet the malicious actions of the humans who slaughtered the beavers are in stark contrast to that animal's intelligence and natural behavior.

A ten-foot-high chain link enclosure surrounded a five-acre area. The fencing was stretched between sturdy twelve-foot lodgepole posts and was cleated to the ground. Across the top were strung four tiers of electric wire for protection.

A five-acre compound comprises a mere corner of a wild cougar's territory, which can cover 150 square miles. For a cougar raised in captivity, however, it is a veritable paradise.

Signs required by the Forest Service keep curious backpackers and horse-back riders at a distance from the enclosure.

After being transported from the Boise Zoo, the hundred-pound Catrina takes her first cautious steps into a world unlike any she has ever known.

It is said that a mountain lion never goes over anything it can go under, but where there's water rules are to be broken.

That wire provided 2,800 volts of low-amperage jolt against escape or break-in. This may seem excessive, but cougars can jump at least ten feet in the air from a standing position, so the barrier was realistically a minimum deterrent.

The site seemed perfect except for one missing essential: a cave, a dark, concealed den for our cougar. With a great variety of natural rock configurations there was not one snug, secluded cavity. My production manager, Jake Provonsha, suggested that we create a den by spanning the five-foot distance between two existing rocks with a man-made rock, thus giving our mountain lion protection from the elements, a sense of security, a roof over its head—such anthropomorphic necessities! Actually, as we understood at this early stage of cougar research, a cave was as necessary as a stream from which to drink—especially if we were to find a pregnant cat who would want to keep her kittens tucked away for approximately two months.

Jake set about the task of fabricating a rock that would blend perfectly in form, color, and surface quality with the existing natural rocks. He constructed a two-by-two wooden skeleton eight feet long, six feet wide, and three feet deep. The frame was covered with metal lathing and encased in lightweight plaster that was painted with a neutral colored acrylic. We moved the "rock" to its position in the enclosure. It rested on granite supports while Jake and my good friend and *National Geographic* illustrator, John Dawson, gave it the colors and textures of its adopted rock family. It was truly a work of art, so harmonious with its surroundings that it was indiscernible. It fooled the eye of anyone we tested to find it among all the other rocks. Now, if it could only fool a cougar.

▾ ▾ ▾

Death is swift for the young elk, and in less than twenty seconds it ceases to struggle. Its mother and the herd have scattered to safety in the dark recesses of the pine forest. Instinctually, they know that the cougar will not pursue them.

There is no reason to. Her meal lies lifeless, a quiescent feast on the damp earth beneath her.

The lion methodically plucks mouthful after mouthful of coarse, tan fur from the underside of the elk. A clump of hair clings to her whiskers and tickles her nose. She shakes her head, brings her left paw to her face, and swipes at the fur. It settles to the ground. Once the skin is bare, she tears open the abdomen and chest cavity by ripping back a strip of flesh. She begins to consume the flavorful viscera.

The lion feasts for several hours till she is no longer hungry. Then she grasps the neck of the carcass in her powerful jaws and drags it thirty feet, over fallen trees and across a small creek to the base of a fir. There, she scratches and paws twigs, pine needles, leaves, and dirt into the stomach cavity and over the remains of the elk to keep it hidden and fresh until she returns in a day or two to eat some more. Researchers indicate that once the carcass is "cached," a mountain lion will stay nearby until it is completely consumed. Depending on the size of the kill, this could take up to two weeks. If the carcass is not closely guarded, scavenger birds— ravens, gray jays, eagles, or magpies—will eat their fill. It is possible that the lion will have to chase another of its own kind from the cache or even kill a smaller predator, like a bobcat, to protect its kill.

Idaho Fish and Game officials tell repeated stories of snowplows unburying cached elk carcasses in the middle of the road after a winter storm. In each instance, they say, it is most likely that a young or inexperienced cougar chased its prey down a steep hillside and brought down the animal on the road. After feeding on the kill, the cougar, in order to avoid hauling the prey up the steep pitch or losing it to the river below, buried it in the road, not expecting human interference.

A thirsty mountain lion laps water from a mountain stream.

3

New Home

Finding a mountain lion with which to grace the miniature habitat we had enclosed was actually easier than I had envisioned, since orphaned cougar kittens are often found by hunters who have shot the mother. Killing female cougars is illegal in some states where cougar hunting is permitted. Montana, for example, has strict regulations to prevent indiscriminate hunting. Idaho has minimal gender restrictions, although lion management is currently tightening regulations on shooting females by means of a quota system similar to Montana's. In any case, the distinction between male and female cougars is extremely difficult to discern. The ears of the male sit lower on the head than they do on the female, and the mature male is considerably larger: an average of 165 pounds compared to 90 to 120 pounds for the female. Even so, an adult female and a year-old male cub can be identical in size and weight, so one can easily be mistaken for the other. Hunters usually leave orphan kittens on the doorstep of fish and game departments or at veterinary clinics where they are nursed and fed until adolescence, then given to a zoo or a private individual. The cougar I was given the opportunity to adopt was one of these—born in the wild and raised in captivity.

Maurice Hornocker knew of two adult mountain lions that the Boise Zoo

A spike-toothed yawn gives evidence of Catrina's many moods.

Catrina sharpens her claws on a gnarly aspen. The cougar's claws are retracted in the pads of the feet except for acceleration, climbing, and grasping prey.

might offer me for the film project. The zoo director, having discovered that the lions' caretaker had doomed them to the taxidermist's knife, brought them to the safety of the zoo until a better home could be found. Since the idea of managing even one mountain lion seemed logistically monumental, two were unthinkable. I was more keen on the four-year-old female because of the possibility that she might be pregnant after living in the same pen with the male.

My film crew and I named our cougar Catrina, and late in June we transported her, secured in a large steel box, to her new home at the foot of the White Cloud Mountains in south central Idaho. In the wild, a male mountain lion will roam fifty to 150 square miles, the female approximately twenty-five to seventy-five square miles of diverse topography and vegetation. However, to our lion, raised in confinement since an early age, this five acres must have seemed limitless.

We initially observed her orientation to these surroundings from outside the enclosure. Protected by the chain link barrier, we were building up enough courage and understanding of her movements and temperament to walk inside and film her. Catrina explored each new element with a hesitation and curiosity equal to my own. As she became more familiar with the novelty of climbing trees, chasing ground squirrels, jumping the creek—sometimes missing her calculation and then shaking off all that nasty water—she assumed an even more astute and elegant demeanor. The exhilaration drew out an innate comprehension and perfect balance with the natural world. Acting on the depths of her instinctual knowledge, she quickly pounced on and killed a ground squirrel, her first prey.

I was fascinated with the cougar's finesse and graceful, silent perfection of motion as I watched her bound, seemingly feather-light, from rock to boulder, seldom travelling in a straight path but committed to a destination. Her sleek, sinuous musculature moved with the effortless power and the graceful ease of an acrobat.

In North America cougars roam a diverse range of habitat, from alpine valleys and Florida swamps to the red rock deserts of the Southwest. Keys to their presence are the availability of prey and sufficient cover.

With a burst of energy, Catrina leaps after a raven she finds stealing her food. Cougars can spring forward twenty-five feet from a standstill, leap twelve feet in the air, and jump safely from a height of sixty feet.

A camouflaged wilderness recluse, the mountain lion often sees humans and retreats rather than reveal itself.

We watched as she raced up the rocky slope and bounded to the crest of the hill. Mountain lions appear to be always seeking a vantage point from which they can observe prey below. It seemed that the film crew was most often the object of Catrina's intense stare.

Her large eyes, amber with a blue-green tint and provocative positioning, glared at us, measuring our worth. From the first days with Catrina to the very last, we never felt totally free of that intense stare, of those eyes that said, "I could put a stop to all this nonsense in a flash if I chose to—but meanwhile, go ahead."

One reason mountain lions are so rarely sighted in the wild is that they usually see a human being long before that person could possibly catch a glimpse of them. Acute vision and a peripheral span in excess of two hundred degrees not only give the cougar a predatory advantage, but also allow it to vanish quickly from humans, its only natural enemy.

Like a ghost it is elusive, appearing, then vanishing, offering only an apparition, an inkling of its existence, paw prints in the snow. Skillfully the lion weaves its camouflaged way through rocky crags, forest ground cover, or sparse sagebrush. Whether furtively stalking its prey or eluding the eye of man, the lion's silence coupled with an earthy coloration allow it to melt into a perfect camouflage with its surroundings—the dried grasses of autumn, the red rocks of the desert Southwest, the orange and green dappling of lichen on textured rock surfaces. It becomes a mirage that is visible one moment and then evanesces into an imperceptible blend with its environment.

Catrina's ability to camouflage, combined with her sudden, electric bursts of velocity and the erratic, unpredictable nature of her personality, made filming her an extraordinarily difficult task. During the first days working with her we were all mindful of our safety—and with good reason. The cougar would stalk and

Catrina rests contentedly amidst sage, wild flowers, and summer grasses.

Although the cougar of the American West now has sufficient space to survive, a remnant population of the Florida panther, the only exist-ing Eastern cougar, has received full legal protection under the Endangered Species Act since 1973.

attack us at every opportunity, and was deterred at the last moment from her springing on us by our holding a large, heavy stick up to her in a defensive gesture and firmly yelling "No!" She would slow her pace to a walk, turn away, and often plop in the shade to rest, as if a nap was all she really wanted in the first place. After a few minutes' rest she would get up, slowly walk away, turn toward us, stalk, and charge again. An unsettling game to say the least, and it forced us to avoid turning our backs on her. One of the crew always made eye contact with her when she appeared in a crouched, stalking pose, and, in most cases, this connection would dissuade Catrina from leaping through the air and landing on someone's back or reaching her paws around a leg to tackle one of us. Our philosophy in dealing with this behavior was that, for Catrina, it was a game like hide-and-seek or tackle football, just a game that sometimes got too rough and too scary for us. It was play that could have led to more, to an uncontrollable urge to test her skills, an unconscious and instinctual desire to go further than playing the game. We were constantly aware that this cougar could kill us in seconds. There were times while I was filming Catrina that she prowled a radius of forty to fifty feet from the camera, concealing herself behind some sagebrush and, just as her image would come into focus, as my vision adjusted to her camouflage, she would spring from position, charge me, stop, and gaze into her mirrored reflection in the camera lens. A moment later she would come to rest at my feet indicating that she had had enough performing for the day. It was time to quit.

As we spent more time in the enclosure filming Catrina's behavior, we began to understand her personality and the vicissitudes of her moods. She was as unpredictable, playful, affectionate, and independent as a domestic cat. She accepted our attention to her; then she wandered away, reticent and indifferent. At times the affection Catrina displayed toward me was almost tender, but I knew she could easily become too ardent. Early on I realized she liked to suck on my fingers. This was okay with me. It was a challenge to let her know that I trusted her. She slowly started to turn the challenge around until my fingers were pulled deeper into the grasp of her powerful jaws and I began to have difficulty getting my hand out of her mouth. I stopped the game, realizing that, for Catrina, affection or any inter-action was welcomed only on her terms.

A description of mountain lion encounters with humans is, at best, puzzling and unpredictable. Like us, their individual behaviorial and personality variations are as many as their numbers, and the most rigid assumptions can be made only of their predatory and reproductive nature. Although the animal's nature is to avoid man, there are legendary native and contemporary anecdotes of individual cats whose curiosity forced them to break the rules. One comes to mind. A Nez Percé woman walking through a forest on her way to visit a friend noticed that a cougar was following her. Once the cat appeared in front of her on the trail, then disap-peared. Sensing the cat was still with her, she looked to either side of the path and found it walking a course parallel to her own. The cat loped off into the woods. Thinking the cougar had finally left her, she rested on a fallen tree. But minutes later the cougar walked right up to the woman, rested its paws on the log and stared at her. Its curiosity satisfied, it turned and bounded away. Comparable occurrences of cougar friendliness are told in Mexico and Central America where the puma leads lost travelers from the jungle or protects them from the jaguar. In Argentina, the puma is called *Amigo del Christiano* because of its gentleness in the presence of humans.

A Pennsylvania gravestone dated 1751 has the image of a cat carved above the name of Phillip Tanner. It is believed to be the earliest documented fatal cougar attack. History presents us a picture of infrequent, even rare instances of fatal

Indigenous people of Puget Sound called the cougar "Fire Cat." They believed that in August of every year the mythical cat carried fire from the Olympic Mountains to the Selkirks, to Rainier, and back, setting the northwest forests ablaze.

attacks on humans by cougars—less than a dozen since the European settlement of North America. But they do occur and they add confusion to our perception of the mountain lion. It is this enigmatic combination—secrecy and curiosity, docility versus savagery, attraction to and fear of humans—that has fueled man's varied response to the cougar.

▼ ▼ ▼

In late February the solitary female lion comes into estrus and, for the first time since leaving her mother and siblings, she craves interaction with another lion. Her sexual maturity came several months ago, but actual reproductive function was suppressed by an innate barrier that could not be lifted until she was socially mature as well. For the welfare of the kittens she would someday raise, she needed to establish residence, to find her own territory. She wandered as a transient in search of a "home" for over a year. Finally, the female found her domain. Now she is desirous of a mate.

The icy hours of daybreak are repeatedly shattered by the lion's solicitous screech. The harsh, perturbing caterwaul sounds like the noise domestic cats make fighting one another in the night. The female persists, as this is her most effective means of capturing the attention of a male with whose territory hers overlaps.

American folklore abounds with stories of the infamous "scream" of the vicious panther. Much of the early settlers' fear of the lion was in response to the unnerving cry that caused women and children to hide indoors while the men, obsessed with a desire to destroy the creature, rode off into the night, armed with rifles. Their fear of the cougar's scream and the unknown not only legitimized killing the animal but it also permitted them to exaggerate their heroics and the beast's hostility. A typical description of the scream justified the pioneers' need to eradicate the source of their fear—in a sense, to kill their own unacceptable weakness:

"The unearthly scream of the panther close at hand will almost freeze the blood in one's veins, and for an instant paralyze almost any form of man or beast." (J. B. Tinsley, *The Puma,* 75.)

The scream, yet another paradox in the cougar's bewildering behavior, is a vocalization limited to females in estrus. Having first heard the sounds of a cougar in estrus at the Olympic Game Farm in Sequim, Washington, my reaction was not one of terror; but, of course, the cat was in a cage and I was not a pioneer on an unknown continent. However, folklore and popular literature have greatly overstated how frequently cougars scream. It is not the common practice of an animal so secretive and ghostly to emit sounds that could potentially frighten away its prey. Hornocker stresses that the predatory existence of the mountain lion is totally dependent on its ability to stalk its prey silently and attack by surprise.

The lion's shrill invitation continues all day long and into the night. Her movements become increasingly serpentine as she travels about her territory. Sometimes she straddles a log and, resting on her forelegs with hindquarters raised, she plows her neck alongside the log and rubs it repeatedly until a moist, viscous fluid is secreted from a gland in her neck. By midnight a six-year-old male approaches one of the scent logs. In an attempt to smell the female's odor he lowers his head to the secretion and raises his nose, allowing air to pass into his pharynx. Curling his lip, he grimaces as if displeased. His behavior allows the smell to pass over a sensory gland in the roof of his mouth so he can "taste" the scent.

The lion courts the female for three days, attempting to initiate copulation by standing close to her back end. She resists and swats him in the face. He withdraws repeatedly, abashed. Even so, she persists in tormenting him. She flicks her tail to one side and presses her hindquarters to his nose or crouches seductively in front of him. Eventually, on the fourth day she accepts his amorous advances.

Lithe and agile, the cougar unfailingly moves with grace.

4

Living with a Lion

For six days the enraptured male pursues his arduous "lovemaking." To induce ovulation and assure the passing of his genes he couples with his mate as often as forty times in a day. As he mounts the female, he gnaws her neck in an affectionate jaw lock. The female, although physiologically receptive, clearly is not blinded by ecstasy. Flattening her ears, she snarls with irritation. After he is finished, the male quickly backs off before his partner swirls around and swats him in the face with her claws. In such adversity, it is a wonder that he persists.

The pair lingers together for several days after copulation. This two-week mating period is the male lion's peak of social tolerance and, although he will mate with other females whose territories intersect his own, the bond with them is equally short-lived. The male will not participate in raising the kittens he has sired. A mutually respected territorial boundary separates the lions, and the distance is maintained by an intuitive awareness of the whereabouts of neighboring lions as well as visual contact, scents, and tracks.

▾ ▾ ▾

The hour-and-a-half drive from my cabin in Ketchum to the cougar enclosure took me past the ten-thousand-foot peaks of the Boulder and Smoky Mountains,

Catrina unpredictably stalked and charged the film crew throughout the entire project. In the wild, cougars shy from humans and very rarely attack.

excellent habitat for elk, deer, mountain goats and the rare wolverine. After scaling Galena Summit, the road descends into the awesome expanse of the Sawtooth Valley, bordered on the west by the serrated granite peaks of the Sawtooth range and on the east by the billowy, alabaster summits of the White Cloud Mountains. These peaks, many of which are unnamed, have a magical appearance from a distance. One summer evening, camped below Mount Cramer in the Sawtooths, I watched the changing light on the White Clouds illuminated by the setting sun. As the sun sank, the chalk walls glowed a radiant citron against the cobalt sky. The yellow melted into a luminous orange afterglow that faded to gray as the light diminished. Suddenly, for only a few seconds, a brilliant turquoise shadow from a smaller mountain was cast on the ghostly peak.

At this latitude and elevation the light in early morning and evening, filtered by the atmosphere, is warmer, richer, and softer than the harsh midday light. This was the light I needed for filming Catrina, which necessitated our setting up a camp to live at the enclosure with our cougar. Another factor in this decision was that Catrina's moods limited our work with her to only one and a half to two hours at a time. Beyond that she would become uneasy and either challenge the crew aggressively or find a cool spot under a tree to take a nap. It was always Catrina's tolerance that determined the extent of our interaction with her.

We set up safari-style tents at the foot of a grassy hill, tucked into the edge of a large aspen grove near the enclosure. The twelve-by-thirty-foot main tent contained a kitchen, the domain of Patty Provonsha. Not only did Patty manage all the cooking, but she also doubled as my camera assistant. All our camera equipment and sound gear was stored in this wall tent, protected from extreme summer heat, dust, and dampness. A work table gave us an area for changing and logging movie and still film, as well as for preparing the packs for a shooting session with the necessary lenses, cameras, film magazines, and miscellaneous gear. On hot days the main tent remained cool and airy; and on cool days and cold nights a wood-stove provided warmth. We lived at "cougar camp" four days a week, returning to town to charge batteries, send off film, view processed film, restock, and take a day off. We followed this routine from May through October for two years.

The camp had two sleep tents, a shielded shower area, and a privy tent. One day Patty burst into the cook tent and told us we had a new visitor in camp. A badger had made her home outside the privy. She had dug a large hole behind a log partially obscured by leafy underbrush and wild geraniums. Patty said the badger, sitting up and staring at her, looked like a tree stump. Laughing, she said, "I don't know what badgers eat, but I hope it's not bare behinds." From then on a trip to the outhouse was dubbed "a visit to the badger."

The badger was not the only wildlife in the area surrounding the camp. Long-eared mule deer summered in the nearby forests and rocky uplands. We frequently saw a herd of twelve to fifteen elk crossing the road leading into camp or making their way up the grass- and sage-covered ridges nearby. Elk is a primary food source for cougars in the Northern Rockies. I am sure Catrina saw the elk, but because she was not raised in the wild and paid little attention to anything outside her confines, she ignored them. Nor did the elk appear to be particularly nervous about the cougar's presence. The behavior on both sides was a mystery to me.

An active family of beavers had created a huge pond just up the creek from the camp. As a result of heavy hunting pressure in the 1800s, when beaver pelts were in great demand to make beaver top hats, the innately diurnal beaver became a nocturnal creature, sleeping in the den all day and emerging to the pond's surface only at night to pursue its industrious dam building and food gathering. I saw the beavers swimming along the banks of the pond several times and was gently reminded of all the beavers I had studied and filmed.

In the pond I saw a river otter the size of an average black Labrador retriever.

From a distance Jim Dutcher catches his elusive subject at play.

Fully outstretched the mountain lion measures up to eight feet, the tail being one third of the total length. In the Western Hemisphere only the jaguar is larger.

A sea of fog settles over Ocalkens Lake as the high peaks of the White Cloud Mountains are illuminated with alpenglow.

A family of green-winged teal with little tufts of downy feathers followed the lead of their mother. The drake of this species is a striking duck with a grass-green, paisley-shaped stripe circling the eye and dividing in half its cinnamon-colored head. A belted kingfisher with punk-style feathers atop a large head made frequent dives from the air into the water, scooping up small trout in its long, sharp beak.

The camp was alive with innumerable songs, calls, warbles, chirps, rattles, whistles, quacks, and trills from sixty or more different species of birds. The dazzling colors of the western tanager dappled the limbs of a willow with brilliant red-orange, yellow, and black, like an impressionist's splattering of paint on canvas.

Mountain bluebirds darted in and out of camp from time to time, tilting their sky-blue plumage to the sunlight. A variety of woodpeckers played rat-a-tat-tat on resonant branches of trees, tent poles, and fence posts. One yellow-bellied sapsucker, drilling a series of tiny holes into an aspen in the enclosure in its search for sap and insects, ended up in Catrina's belly. I found the half-eaten remains of the small bird one day, and the next day only a few patterned feathers remained on the ground.

Narrow trails cut paths from one tent to another, and the most important rule of the camp was that these paths were used between tents to avoid unnecessary trampling of fragile vegetation. At seven thousand feet the growing season is short; cool temperatures and the possibility of snowfall even during summer months make plants especially vulnerable. Most visitors to the site were attentive to this precept, and impact was kept to a minimum. However, we were all awakened one mid-June morning to the ceaseless *baa...baa...*of thousands of sheep moving their way right through camp! They surrounded the tents like a dense fog. Soon enough Carlos, the Peruvian sheepherder, came along, unperturbed that his band of sheep, while straying up the canyon to find some greener, tastier grass, had swarmed around our camp, trampling wildflowers and destroying the precious greenery we so carefully protected. Carlos was equally oblivious to the clearly delineated pathways, but he was good-natured and happy to have someone with whom he might converse. He chattered away in Spanish while I recognized a few words here and there. There was no way I could explain about the paths, but I had no trouble convincing him to direct his sheep back down the canyon. All I had to do was point to the cougar on the other side of the fence twenty yards away.

These several thousand grazing sheep were following the open corridors of public lands. In the late 1870s and 1880s ranchers appropriated vast amounts of western lands for the purpose of grazing livestock. As a result, two hundred and forty million acres of virgin grassland were depleted, degraded, or destroyed. The industry flourished and prosperous ranchers soon controlled the political climate of the early West. Many of the laws and grazing practices established by the live-stock industry a hundred years ago stand strong today, and now nearly half the land area in eleven western states is owned by the American public and virtually all of it can be used by private ranchers.

This long-term practice has weakened the habitat and fragile ecosystems that sustain indigenous animals like the mountain lion. Contamination of streams, soil erosion, and destruction of native vegetation all combine to endanger the con-tinued existence of countless plant and animal species.

Not only is the cougar threatened by the loss of habitat as a result of livestock grazing, but lions, especially those that prey on sheep and cattle, are eliminated. Because the Bureau of Land Management (BLM) permits ranchers to use public lands, livestock are grazed in remote areas known to be prime cougar habitat. Calves born on isolated rangelands are easy pickings for the cougar. Not only is livestock raised on the cougar's predatory doorstep, but its grazing can reduce for-age, resulting in a scarcity of elk and deer, the cougar's primary prey.

Researchers consider depredation by cougars to be generally confined to phys-

Mottled granite rocks form a maze of hideouts for Catrina as well as the photographer.

Dubbed "Cougar Camp," the film crew's base of operations serves as a comfortable home six months of the year for two years.

ically subnormal animals—the old, inexperienced, or wounded lion that might kill in a frenzy. In reality, lion depredation is infrequent. Statistics show, for example, that from June 1986 to July 1987 cougars killed 5 percent of all the sheep in the United States lost to predators. Coyotes were responsible for 78 percent and domestic dogs for 11 percent.

Even so, historical pressure from the livestock industry forced the federal government to establish special predator control programs. Initiated in the 1890s as the Predator and Rodent Control Agency, Animal Damage Control (the ADC) has been successful in eliminating the wolf and the grizzly from most western states. Coyotes are currently the main victims, with a hundred thousand killed annually. Two hundred mountain lions were killed by the ADC in 1988. These extremely expensive programs (funded by taxpayers) have nondestructive alternatives. Many ranchers are switching from cow-calf to steer operations in areas of high loss. They are building electric fences and using guard dog breeds to dissuade predators from attacking their cattle or sheep.

Meanwhile, Catrina completely ignored the waves of walking mutton, not at all tantalized by their pungent odor or provoked by their pathetic bleating. As a lifetime captive animal, this cougar preferred a turkey leg to a leg of lamb. Jake was in charge of feeding her, a chore simultaneously mundane and adrenalin-surging. As the meat was being prepared, she paced the fence impatiently. Sometimes, just as Jake was about to toss a piece over the fence, Catrina would thrust her paw with mercurial speed, claws fully extended, through the narrow opening between the gate and fence, snarling and growling. Once, she climbed this section of twelve-foot fence as the meat was thrown up in the air. In a matter of seconds the hundred-pound mountain lion was five feet above Jake's head. We realized then that Catrina could scale the fence anytime she wanted to check out the other side.

Catrina's feline curiosity prompted her to investigate any new piece of gear, loose clothing, or props that we brought into the enclosure. One day as we were about to leave camp, Jake decided to store his and Patty's mountain bikes inside the enclosure for safekeeping from potential camp intruders—the human sort. As he rested the bikes against the fence, he noticed that Catrina was curious but not aggressively interested in them. She sniffed them and walked away. Just as I was about to drive off, I looked back at her and saw, to my astonishment, that she was ripping the bicycle seats to shreads. She tore off the leather, and all that remained were the bare metal skeletons of this strange beast that she found not quite tasty or malleable enough to devour.

Mountain lions are notorious for their ability to camouflage. Here, Catrina as copycat carries the notoriety too far.

5

Cougar Kittens

The greening weeks of June waned into July, when desert-hot days built a barricade of high pressure against rain-bearing clouds. Idaho was smack in the middle of a scorching drought and the days brought igneous heat like the temperatures cast off by an enormous bonfire. And still the wildflowers continued to display their colorful array. Tuliplike, white mariposa lilies and periwinkle blue lupine speckled the sparse, gray-green sagebrush landscape.

Near the end of the second week in July, Catrina still gave no obvious indications that she was about to give birth. Instead of our anticipated changes in weight, appetite, and temperament, the only apparent difference was that she seemed very sensitive to the scorching heat. She spent most of her time in the shade of a tree, panting to lower her body temperature.

Late one afternoon, as we entered the enclosure to begin filming, Catrina was nowhere to be found. We searched for forty-five minutes, hoping to find her tucked away in a dark hideout giving birth. We checked the cool north side, all the rocky crevices and hideaways, the nests of grasses beneath twinberry bushes on the far east side, and the darker retreats in conifers by the creek. Passing the artificial rock a third time, we started down the hill. Suddenly, we heard Catrina's chirping call and turned to see her standing by the upper end of the rock. Turning, she vanished.

A cougar kitten's spots, vestigial remains of its ancestral species, mask the young until they are six months old.

In mid-July Catrina gave birth to three tiny kittens. Twenty-four hours after they were born she began moving them from one location to another, presumably in response to temperature fluctuations.

At two weeks old, Spook, Casper, and Marley are just gaining enough strength in their wobbly limbs to venture a few steps from the den.

Mother cougars nurse their young fifteen minutes after birth until the kittens are capable of eating meat at two months. Total weaning may not occur until the cub is six months old.

We climbed the hill, but Catrina was gone. We heard her chirp again. This time from *inside* the rock.

Peering through a small opening at the end of the rock, I saw Catrina's pale apricot color dim in the surrounding darkness. I shone a flashlight in to determine if there were any kittens by her side, but all I could see was the tight maze of internal framework.

When we designed the rock, we figured it would be wedged between natural rocks. Consequently, to minimize the weight, Jake left the ends open. Camera angles would not reveal that area of the rock. When we placed it in position, a portion of the upper opening was left exposed, forming a small crevice that Catrina ripped to a hole large enough to let her body pass.

Catrina refused to leave the rock's interior.

It was obvious she planned to give birth inside the rock. Her decision presented us with a disturbing problem—mostly of our own doing, as we had created the ersatz rock. Catrina's weight had begun to break a hole in the floor of the structure. In her anxiety over the nature of her den, she was tearing the hole even larger.

Accepting that we could not thwart her desperate intentions, we left her, but only twenty minutes later, her loud cat yowl brought us running back to the rock.

Again I took a flashlight and peered into the darkness. The beam of light revealed a tiny kitten next to Catrina. As I watched, she gave birth to a second.

We left her a bowl of water and some food on the ground beneath the rock. The situation was now worse. Not only were the cougar kittens born inside the rock and away from camera view, but they lay perilously close to the jagged metal and gaping hole through which one could easily tumble to the ground below.

Fortunately, the following morning, we found Catrina resting calmly with

A spotted kitten emerges from a tangled thicket of fallen trees that serves as a den.

Distracted, Catrina appears to ignore the summons of her youngster. However, cougar mothers do have an intricate system of audible and inaudible communication with their kittens.

her two kittens inside the rock. But, while checking the condition of the dilapi-dated structure, I discovered a third kitten on the ground, covered with blood, its umbilical cord still attached and wrapped around a sage bush. The tiny creature had survived the cool mountain night, away from its mother for possibly fourteen hours. I cut the umbilical cord and handed the kitten to Catrina. She took it in her mouth and began to lick its spotted fur.

Cougar kittens can be born at any time of the year. However, in northern lati-tudes, the breeding period is limited to late winter and early spring. This allows the kittens to be born, after an average ninety-two-day gestation period, into a warmer and more hospitable climate. Their survival rate is higher than it would be if they arrived into the severity of a mountain winter. A cave, windfall, or brushy area beneath a rocky ledge serves as a den, provided that the space is protected from weather and harsh light. Newborn mountain lion kittens weigh between twelve and sixteen ounces and are born with their eyes closed. Litter sizes can be as large as six kittens, but the average is two or three. They begin to nurse within an hour of birth and a day later competitive behavior starts with a blind struggle for the teat. Their pale tawny coats are dappled with penny-sized patches of darker fur. Streaks of the same color ring the face, legs, and tiny tail. This ancestral patterning of fur blends a kitten into the lights and darks of its multicolored surroundings.

After leaving Catrina alone with her kittens for a day, we returned to the rock the following morning only to find it empty. Catrina had obviously moved them, but we were startled. Most of the literature I had read indicated that a mother will keep her young hidden in the den for almost two months. Moments later we found her lying in the morning sun next to a large rock nursing her three kittens. She was panting and had a distracted, indolent look. Although the heat was oppressive to her, instinct evidently told her that the tiny newborns needed warmth.

A guarded, blue-eyed kitten takes refuge from the camera and hides behind his mother's legs. Cougar kittens learn caution as a defensive measure against predators—wolverine, bobcat, eagle, and owl.

Newborn cougar kittens weigh less than one pound at birth. At maturity, male lions can weigh between one hundred and eighty and two hundred pounds.

Catrina takes her kittens on an exploratory journey. In the wild, youngsters must have the strength and agility to travel to kill sites at eight weeks.

I shot two rolls of movie film as the kittens eagerly suckled. As each one pulled its wet muzzle away from the nipple, Catrina lapped milk from its pudgy face, a motion that soothed the kitten to sleep. One by one Catrina began to move them again—this time to a slightly cooler location at the base of a fir tree. To transfer each kitten, the mother gently wrapped her powerful jaws around its delicate head and carried its limp body to a new bed.

As I was about to run out of film, I asked my soundman, Peter, to make a trip to town to bring a new supply. While he was gone, I lay down on the ground, resting my head and shoulders against a rock to take a nap. Either I looked to Catrina like an inviting pillow or else she just wanted some affection after her ordeal of the last twenty-four hours. She tried to stretch her hundred pounds over the length of my relaxed body, gently tapping her head against mine several times—a feline form of greeting. As flattering as her fervent attentions were, she was also heavy! I pushed her aside and she laid down next to me for a joint nap. When I awoke, she was gone. She had left to move her kittens again, following the track of the sun.

This moment of tranquility and time alone with Catrina established a mutual respect and a bond of understanding between us. As I leaned against the rock and permitted her to lay her powerful body over mine, she found my angle of repose, the settling of my tensions. From that moment on, Catrina expressed an affection for me and seemed to seek my presence as a form of refuge when she tired from the pressure of the filming sessions.

I can only speculate why Catrina moved her offspring so often; several times each day for a week and then once every three or four days for two months. Temperature was a factor, especially when they were very young and immobile. I also think that as the den was soured by urine, Catrina instinctually carried her kittens away from the nest where its odor could, in the wild, attract dangerous attention from other predators. I considered the mother might move the litter frequently because of the film crew's daily disturbance, but, each time we entered the enclosure, Catrina led us directly to her kittens.

At ten days the kittens' violet-blue eyes were open, and by two weeks their large heads bobbed from tiny bodies atop legs too short and wobbly to support their burden. They were the antithesis of the graceful feline elegance of their mother. We were able to distinguish one from another and decided to give them names that reflected the cougar's ghostly nature. The darkest we named Spook, as it was the most easily startled. The heftiest and most aggressive was a pale, strawberry blond with barely visible spots. We named this one Marley after Scrooge's former partner who comes back to haunt him in Dickens's *Christmas Carol*. We called the smallest kitten Casper. I always thought this was probably the little guy I found lying on the ground the morning after its birth. As the kittens later developed their own personalities, Casper seemed most needy of Catrina while the other two banded together, more aloof and suspicious of our actions.

They began to make their way clumsily over twigs and pebble-sized rocks in a six-foot radius from their den. When Catrina was with them, this exploration was permitted; but when she wanted them in the den, she would fetch them, one at a time in her mouth, settle them with a generous lapping of the tongue, and give them a silent command to stay put. There they would remain while Catrina left to investigate our activities or seek a respite from her demanding litter. The cougar kitten's survival depends on its obedience to this nonvocal message. Venturing away from a protected site while the mother is off hunting could be an open invitation to a hungry bear, wolverine, bobcat, eagle, or coyote.

All the same, a naive courage and newfound strength in their little legs carried them farther from the den each day. Many times a kitten suddenly found itself all alone in a hostile world with no warm mother in sight. Blue eyes glistening and head trembling, it would cry out for her with a desperate, rasping whistle, like the

70

screech of a hawk. Catrina responded in a chirping summons—a medium-pitched, staccato meow. She used a similar sound to greet me when I approached the gate to the enclosure after a few days away from camp. By the time the kittens were two months old, the whistle evolved into a richer, louder sound that had an almost ventriloquial quality—seeming to come from one place and then another. Once quieted by Catrina's approach and gentle licking, the kitten was carried back to the rest of the family.

▾ ▾ ▾

Early one evening in August, before the sun has left the high ridges but after the valleys have succumbed to shadows, a burly young black bear lumbers through a tree-fringed meadow. He stops often, stuffing his long snout into anthills or helping himself to a bounty of sweet serviceberries. He swats annoying mosquitoes from his nose and swings his shiny brown head to and fro as if the motion gives him momentum. Abruptly he stands on his two hind legs and throws his snout into the air. Growling nervously, he runs into the trees.

The female mountain lion, sitting alongside a log farther up the draw, perks her ears as she spots the bear and follows him with keen eyes as he turns into the forest. She bounds after him, leaving behind the tranquility of the evening. In the striated cover of aspens they clash for several minutes—a melee of charges, retreats, challenges, growls, and snarls. The bear emerges from the trees chased by the cougar. He keeps running. Confident that her massive adversary has been frightened away, she halts and looks uphill. Two pairs of blue eyes timidly peer over the curve of the log. Their mother chirps as she approaches. The ten-week-old kittens scramble from their hiding place and are greeted by their mother's affectionate coo.

"Twins" Casper and Marley become astute observers of their surroundings.

6

Education for Survival

The cougar family's den, not far up the hill, is hidden beneath a granite outcrop that is part of a stepping-stone formation of ledges, crevices, and cliffs. Surrounded by a dense growth of conifers and understory brush, it looks out freely on the long vista of the valley floor.

As the female and her young travel the short distance back to their den, the sun-gilded summits dissolve in fading light. To the west, alpine contours are sharpened into dusky, backlit silhouettes. The frisky kittens follow close behind their mother, running and stumbling forward on hefty legs and paws that seem cumbersome and clumsy. They do not stray from their mother's path. It is too late in the evening for plucky adventurism.

Their mother stops and stares at a dark mound hunched on a tree trunk. Turning to her kittens, she silently signals them to stay put, then slinks slowly toward the tree. Aware of danger, the animal scuttles higher up into branches, but it is too late. The cougar leaps into the air. With one swipe of her paw, she throws the animal to the ground. The animal arches its back, erects its spines, and lashes out at its tormentor with its heavily quilled tail. A puzzling form of defense frustrates the cougar's attack. She swiftly swats and nudges the porcupine, cautiously

Drenched from a duck chase, Catrina takes on a bizarre and fierce appearance as she attempts to call her kittens to the kill with a mouthful of feathers.

attempting to avoid the spiny armor while trying to roll the animal onto its back so its soft underside is exposed. Her adversary thrashes its tail mercilessly into her snout, scattering forty or fifty barbed quills deep into the flesh. The cougar flinches with pain and frustration. However, in seconds she immobilizes the porcupine in the grip of her claws and tears into its unprotected belly with her teeth. She raises her bloody, quilled head and sharply chirps for her kittens who emerge from their hideout and run to her side.

▾ ▾ ▾

As the middle of August approached, I noticed the cacophony of birdlife had diminished. The chicks of the warbling vireo, the house wren, and yellow-bellied sapsucker had fledged and were now seeking to fill their own stomachs. As much as I enjoy birdwatching, I welcomed the silence. The high-pitched hissing of young sapsuckers, perpetually in demand of food, had sounded like the constant swinging of a squeaking gate.

At four weeks Catrina's kittens were still totally dependent on her for nourishment, warmth, security, and the lengthy process of education that would prepare them to leave her side after twelve to twenty months and begin their solitary struggle for survival. As early as two weeks old, walking feebly on bowed legs, the kittens stalked grasshoppers and blowing grasses. Now they seemed to regard their mother as a giant jungle gym. They climbed all over her, bit her ears (tiny needles of teeth began to appear a week earlier), pulled and swatted her tail. Sometimes a kitten climbed up on top of Catrina's head, nuzzled her ears, and then, spotting a littermate, it pounced from its mountainous perch and tumbled to the ground. At the same time a third kitten might swipe and bat Catrina's snakelike

tail as she flicked it back and forth. Their mother not only tolerated these games,
but joined in.

For all young predator species in the animal kingdom, the most necessary part of their education is play-fighting. Their play—stalking, pouncing, chasing, and tackling—is the rehearsal for survival in the wild. Although cougars are born with this information, they need to develop their competitive spirit and sharpen the skills necessary to bring down moving prey.

The little cougars' mock battles grew progressively more competitive as they gained strength, agility, and speed. They played a rough and tumble game of ambush, hide-and-seek, and tug of war—attacking, scratching, biting, sliding, rolling on the ground, hissing and spitting at one another. As the kittens became more aggressive, they challenged their mother's patience with clawed swipes to her face and frequent assaults on her tail. She was the target for a barrage of juvenile torment. At times, composure gave way to reprimand and she swatted back or growled. The kittens retreated, their puckish spirits temporarily dampened.

For seven weeks, Catrina carried her kittens by the scruff of the neck, often bringing them into camera view. Until they were six weeks they acquiesced. There was an occasional hiss, especially from Marley, when he flashed his miniature, toothpicklike teeth. But his immature belligerence was only slightly threatening because his bright blue eyes sparkled with innocence. Hiding on rock perches or under the arched trunk of a large fallen fir that became their special den, they snarled and hissed whenever any one of the film crew approached. Then they took off running, slinking close to the ground as if that made them invisible. Stealth and evasion, the cougar's most subtle weapons, are learned at an early age.

As brave and independent as these snarling upstarts pretended to be, they were still dependent on the wiles of their mother—and would be for many months.

A doomed mallard pair flees as Catrina bounds into the water. Acutely fixed on her prey, the cougar races to and fro using her tail for balance.

Powerful hind legs thrust Catrina into a final lunge for the mallard.

The cougar springs from the pond, proudly clutching her kill.

Casper remained the most visible to us, as he followed Catrina and responded more often to her chirping summons.

At first we assumed that the kittens would become too accustomed to the presence of humans and to captivity, and we would have no choice but to send them to a zoo at the culmination of the project. However, their own behavior gave us some different ideas. They were obviously "wild," even in an enclosure, and wanted nothing to do with us. Indeed, they were openly pugnacious and hostile on the rare occasions when we saw them at all. With Maurice Hornocker's approval, we made a decision to release Spook, Casper, and Marley into the wild the following spring. They would be nearly a year old then and there would be plenty of rodents on which the young cougars could practice their hunting skills before tackling more substantial prey.

The decision critically affected our logistics. Now we would have to feed not one but four lions through the winter. Also, to give them the best chance at survival once they were set free, we would have to make sure that their mother adequately trained them in hunting skills.

Until mountain lion kittens are eight weeks old, they survive solely on maternal nourishment. By the eighth week their digestive system, teeth, and strength are developed enough for them to travel to a kill site and consume small amounts of flesh. Although weaning begins at two months, most kittens continue to nurse for another month and some until they are half grown. Their period of dependency is lengthy in comparison to that of other predators' offspring, but it serves to regulate the species' numbers and to avoid overpopulation, which could deplete its food supply. The female does not come into estrus as long as her young are dependent (up to twenty months). In short, kittens provide their mother with a sort of built-in birth control that maintains ecologic stability and allows them a better chance at survival.

We began helping Catrina teach her young by supplying her with fresh road-killed rabbits and deer so the kittens could taste wild meat. In autumn, the deer herds migrate from the Boulder, White Cloud, and Sawtooth Mountains to the open prairies and grasslands to the south. Their traditional migration corridors are now intercepted in places by paved highways. Each year thousands of deer are hit and killed by automobiles in Idaho alone.

The first time we fed a road-killed fawn to Catrina, we watched and filmed as she meticulously ripped fur away from the hide, opened the leg, and summoned her nine-week-old kittens, who watched from a safe distance. Casper was the first to appear while Catrina chirped with growing impatience until the two shyer cubs made their way down from the rock hideout, cautiously stalking the carcass. They began to feed, pulling out eyes, chewing on ears—not the most delectable parts of the animal, but the first to attact their attention. One kitten grabbed a huge wad of fur in his mouth. He choked and spit it out. Another dove his head into the torn hindquarter and emerged drenched with blood up to his black muzzle marks. As each of the kittens finished eating, Catrina cleaned it—rolling a kitten onto its back, she pinned it down with her massive paw and licked its face and white belly with her sandpaper tongue.

Catrina dragged the carcass off to a shady location under the boughs of a tree to cache the remains. As she was scraping twigs and dirt over the dead animal, Marley was standing on top of the fawn working hard to undo his mother's efforts.

A week later, after feasting on a road-killed doe, Catrina started to bury the carcass. This time her kittens correctly mimicked their mother's strokes, helping her scratch dirt, leaves, and pine needles into the stomach cavity.

Because direct observation of familial interaction between mountain lions is extremely rare, researchers usually "see" behavior through radio-telemetry signals or by deciphering tracks left in the snow. This inaccessibility to seeing creates a separateness between the cougar's secret world, the scientist's methodical inspection of that world, and the nonscientist's emotional plea for its protection. In circumstances closely approaching the lion's natural world, we established a sense of affinity. We were privileged to observe the kittens' imitation and to visually record previously unseen cougar behavior. Recognizing the privilege, we hoped that our work with these cougars might contribute to an understanding of the mountain lion's threatened placement in the fragile balance of the ecosystem.

Cougar predation, although infrequently observed, is the behavior most understood by the scientific community. In North America, deer and elk are the lion's primary prey. Bighorn sheep and an occasional moose constitute additional large prey. Because the cougar is a solitary predator, its method of killing involves stealth as opposed to open attack, surprise instead of chase. It is a prodigious predator, described by Hornocker as "the epitome of a finely tuned hunting animal. It's like an African lioness single-handedly bringing down a cape buffalo. For sheer killing ability, I don't think any cat in the world surpasses the mountain lion."

The cougar kills a large animal every twelve to fourteen days. A female with kittens, especially in their second winter, places a higher demand on the prey base. A family can devour a deer overnight, consuming all but the teeth, hooves, hide, and sometimes the rumen or parts of the viscera. Most of the bones are crushed, ingested, and later excreted after passing through the short digestive system typical of many carnivores. After the spring snowmelt, following a winter of feeding roadkills to our lions, we curiously came upon clusters of crumbly, chalk-white feces deposited all over the enclosure.

Contrary to popular belief and the mountain lion's remarkable hunting skill, the result of their hunt is by no means assured. For the lion, an ungulate can present a formidable challenge. An eight-hundred-pound bull elk displays a striking

Catrina drops her prize and summons her young with a sharp, staccato meow. Moments later two kittens play tug of war with the carcass. Unlike wolf puppies, who establish pack dominance over prey, the cougar kittens will share the meal agreeably.

Blood and blue-eyed innocence.

rack of potentially lethal antlers. These weapons, along with the animal's powerful kick, much larger size, and greater endurance, constitute an arsenal of defense
that can make the cougar's attack futile or even fatal. The cougar might recognize
the disadvantages to stalking an elk with antlers, and it might select a less dangerous victim without antlers nearby. Females with kittens are more likely to suffer
accidental deaths because of the pressure to feed their young. Hornocker believes
that particularly young, less experienced lions, when attacking elk in steep and
rugged terrain, might be injured or killed in the struggle. Researchers in Utah
once discovered a cougar skull pierced by a branch of curleaf mountain mahogany.
They speculated that the lion was thrown onto the spear of wood when battling
with its prey.

Cougars do not selectively kill only the old, the young, and the infirm—the
cullings of the herd. They attack the animals that are most open to attack. The victim's vulnerability involves physical, biological, and ecological factors that expose
a specific animal to attack. Survival depends on more than physical superiority.

Although it is evident that the cougar does not consistently kill the weak,
its predatory behavior strengthens ungulate populations by controlling overpopulation, which can lead to overgrazing and massive die-offs as a result of insufficient forage. Yellowstone Park is a perfect example of the consequences of
insufficient predatory behavior. Earlier in this century wolves were eliminated
from the park, and currently there is only a small lion population. In the sixties,
because of overpopulation, five thousand elk were shot by park officials. During
the winter of 1988–1989 almost half of an excessive elk population starved to death
as a result of a scarcity of winter forage.

Cougars are opportunistic predators and fancy an eclectic diet that varies
according to season, availability, appetite, and hunting skill. In the summertime

they can survive on small prey: mice, chipmunks, ground squirrels, rabbits, ducks, wood rats, beavers, badgers, and even porcupines. Like wolves and domestic dogs, they eat grass occasionally to reduce parasites in their intestines.

In late September we found the remains—feathers and viscera—of a wild duck that must have landed on the pond inside the enclosure. Catrina had killed and eaten it. Realizing that this had been a perfect opportunity for the cougar to teach her kittens the purpose of all their training, we decided to introduce some stock-raised mallards to the pond.

Released from the pen that held her while the ducks were put in the pond, Catrina wandered from the far northwest corner of the enclosure toward the creek and the quacking mallards. As she approached, she spotted them and immediately sank to the ground. Veiled by cougar-colored grasses, she intently eyed her unsuspecting prey. She rose to a crouch. Never forsaking her stare, she snaked forward with skillful deception. The ducks remained oblivious. In an instant, she dashed into the water. In a haphazard blitz she ran back and forth chasing the startled, fleeing ducks. As four flew off, she vaulted after them with balletic ease, leaving the water twelve feet below. She grasped unsuccessfully and fell to the pond where she spotted two ducks hiding in grasses on the water's edge. Pouncing, she pinned one underwater with her clawed forepaw. Dunking her head below the surface, she grasped the duck in her jaws and sprang to dry ground. Millions of luminescent drops of water sparkled in the sunlight as Catrina convulsively shook her legs and body to eliminte the moisture that penetrated her coat. She began to pluck the duck's downy feathers from its limp body. They floated upward first and then settled like flowers on blades of grass. Catrina paused, turned from her kill, and called her three cubs.

Because a female cougar with kittens must kill more frequently than a solitary cat, she is an extremely opportunistic hunter. Consequently, she leaves more tracks for humans who hunt her.

7

The Hunt

The mountain lion, the most skillful of America's great predators, sits at the pinnacle of its evolutionary pyramid. Nevertheless, it has an enemy whose artifice has managed to extirpate it from most of its ancestral ranges. Ever since the coming of the European colonists, the cougar, puma, panther, or mountain lion has been a predator preyed upon by civilization. The lion's legacy—wilderness—has been victim to a systematic and uninterrupted desolation. Road building, deforestation, mining, hunting, urban expansion, industrial and agricultural development, poaching, and backcountry recreation all combine to challenge the lion's territorial stability and contribute to its demise. This rapid increase in contemporary human interference poses the greatest threat yet to the cougar. However, for three hundred years hunting has been unquestionably the most critical factor in cougar mortality.

Historically, lions were hunted for a variety of reasons which were, in essence, a display of man's need to control his environment. Fear of the unknown and fear of the legendary cougar—hostile, malicious, and bloodthirsty—made killing a culturally accepted motive for protection from the creatures that threatened human survival and the survival of livestock. Cougars were killed because they destroyed private property, the early settler's wager on a new life.

Native Americans esteemed the mountain lion for its stealth and respected it as a guardian spirit.

The skills of survival—stalking, charging, and attacking—must be practiced from an early age. As a lone hunter the mountain lion cannot rely on others as the wolf might.

Indiscriminate hunting of predators and all wildlife prevailed as the pioneers grasped the notions of manifest destiny and stewardship of the land. These early American commandments, the unspoken rules of New World moral conduct, justified killing as a means to tame the wild spaces for human inhabitants. Forests were cleared, crops were planted. Animal life was pressured to move on as its habitat was eliminated. By 1900 the cornucopia of wildlife and fisheries in the eastern woods was radically diminished. The cougar was virtually extinct. And man moved westward, repeating his persecution.

The killing of cougars became a symbol of prestige. Death had conquered fear, and fearless hunters wore the pelts of dead cougars as a mark of distinction and bravery. "Painter" meat was claimed to be tastier than beaver tail or the tender pieces of buffalo. Plains hunters, called wolfers, shot the buffalo, poisoned its meat, and returned the following day to find the carcasses of predators lying dead next to the buffalo—wolf, bobcat, coyote, and cougar.

As early as 1680, states rewarded hunters for their killing by offering a bounty for the pelt of the lion that preyed on livestock and depleted the deer herds. Although the Native American intimately respected the cougar for its hunting skills and considered the cougar and its prey to be one, living in a symbiotic relationship, the European American saw the lion as a competitor for deer. "For the sake of the deer supply," argued *Forest and Stream* magazine in 1885, "the panther should be systematically pursued and destroyed, and the bounty should be such as to encourage this." To this end, the federal government at one time employed two hundred hunters just to kill mountain lions. The lions were destroyed—with guns, traps, and poison.

The last bounties were collected in the 1960s, when it became evident that the extent of lion depredation had been exaggerated and bounty hunters were not selectively killing offenders, but entire families of cougars. Additionally, Americans' values were changing. Wildlife was beginning to receive the respect that was previously given to those who killed it. Approximately sixty-seven thousand cougars were killed from 1917 through the bounty period that ended in the sixties and the free hunt that was halted completely in 1974, when the last state reclassified the mountain lion from "varmint" to "big game" animal. A period of fifty-seven years.

After centuries of vital traditional and cultural reasons for killing cougars—fear, protection, depredation, money—the contemporary justification of sport is frivolous in comparison. During the 1990–1991 season over eighteen hundred cougars were killed legally in the ten states that allow hunting.

In the first days of filming Catrina, I received a copy of an advertisement from the *San Francisco Chronicle* that shouted out in a two-inch bold headline, "ENOUGH!" The ad, paid for by the Sacramento-based Mountain Lion Coalition, berated senseless trophy hunting of lions and asked that Californians support the effort to reinstate the state's moratorium on cougar hunting. In 1971, concerned over the lion's dwindling numbers, the legislature and Governor Reagan placed the first statewide ban on sport hunting of mountain lions.

Realizing the growing interest in the debate over lion hunting, I decided to find an outfitter in Idaho who would be willing to be filmed during an actual hunt. I started negotiations with a guide, Todd Moliter, whose name had been given to me by the Idaho Department of Fish and Game. After I described the film project, Moliter agreed to let me film his hunting operation, but added that he would have to find a client who would cooperate.

Moliter is licensed to guide mountain lion hunts in both the southern hills of Idaho and northern Nevada. He told me that his clients come from all over the

Catrina calls the kittens to a high lookout.

Safe from hunters' guns in her enclosure, Catrina gives a wide, toothy yawn of complacence.

Although some states have restrictions against killing female cougars, most do not. Each time a female is shot, it is likely that she leaves behind two to six kittens who also become victims because they are too young to survive on their own.

United States and as far away as Turkey. I had heard that Europeans travel to this country to hunt elk and deer, but I was astounded to learn that America's lion is considered a hunting prize worldwide.

Lion hunting seasons vary in duration and in regulations in the ten western states where hunting is permitted. Some states allow a year-round hunt in certain districts. Others limit the hunt to a quota system where the district is closed once a specified number of females have been taken. Management practices in certain states are beginning to reflect the understanding that the stability of regional populations is threatened by excessive hunting of female lions. Research shows that a female with small kittens is more likely to be shot than a male, because she leaves an extensive network of visible tracks as she hunts more frequently and returns often to her young. When a hunter kills a nursing female, he also takes the life of her dependent kittens.

Idaho has two designated mountain lion seasons. There is a "pursuit only" period from the end of January to the end of February, where photographers, hunters interested in the chase, or outfitters working their dogs can track down a cat and pursue it with hounds who tree it. The animal is not shot, but is needlessly harassed. The general sport or "take" season opens statewide in early September and can run as late as March 31, depending on the district. Moliter told me that his hunts begin toward the end of November, when snow conditions allow easier tracking. Ideal tracking in snow-covered terrain can assure a 90 percent success rate in treeing and shooting a cougar. Moliter also takes clients at this time, after the deer and elk seasons, because he is permitted to use his bloodhounds.

The cougar has an innate fear of dogs—barking dogs. It will run from a barking dog and climb the nearest tree to escape. Paradoxically, it is perfectly capable of killing a canine in seconds, as two friends and their doberman discovered in a fatal encounter. On a warm spring day in 1977, my friends hiked up a narrow gulch about five miles from the nearest house. Their dog, Amroth, circled them and ran ahead, sniffing the ground and chasing chipmunks. She sniffed once too often, nosing the long tail of a mountain lion that was sleeping in the shade of a bush below a steep cliff. The lion swung around and pounced on Amroth. Around and around in a tight whirlwind of battle they fought. My friends shouted, trying to frighten off the cougar, which was now on top of the dog, finishing her fatal attack. When one of my friends made eye contact with the lion, it took off up to a granite ledge only seventy-five feet away. From this perch it rested for several minutes, watching below. Amroth had one tooth mark on her neck where the cougar had severed the spinal column.

Moliter's three-month schedule was completely booked with week-long hunting excursions for clients who each paid him $2,500 and a small license fee to the Idaho Department of Fish and Game, which sells an unlimited number of mountain lion licenses each year. (For the 1990–1991 hunt the state sold 1,357 cougar licenses, plus an additional 2,968 resident sportsman licenses, which include cougar.) Moliter's first client of the season came from New York for his mountain lion. Although he chose not to be filmed, he boasted about killing three cougars that year, each in a different state. Also, in his hunting career he had "bagged" over a hundred bears. In a strange twist of values, as fear of extinction is rallying people worldwide in an unprecedented effort to save threatened and endangered species, it is also working to create a frenzied competition for record trophies.

A client willing to cooperate with our filming was found and we agreed to meet the hunters at a truck stop in southern Idaho at 4:00 A.M. on December 3. Turning into the parking lot, we saw two pickup trucks loaded with snowmobiles and dog kennels. One of the kennels was equipped with a sled so the dogs could be towed behind a snowmobile while the hunters searched long distances for a

Snarls and retreat suggest little tolerance for the film crew.

fresh cougar track. Nearby, Moliter, a bristle-bearded man in his late thirties who holsters his pistol between his legs, talked with his client, Neil, and an assistant. After hasty introductions, we departed for the hunt.

We followed the two trucks for forty-five minutes along a paved road. As they turned into the rolling sagebrush hills of a wide canyon, the drivers slowed down to look for lion tracks. Soon Moliter stopped his truck, got out, and, after lowering a ramp to the road and unloading a snowmobile, he drove off in a shimmering curtain of snow in search of tracks. Twenty minutes later we heard the whine of his returning snow machine. No tracks had been sighted, even though the ground was covered with a two-inch crust of snow. The only animals he had seen were a lone bobcat and a large herd of mule deer grazing on the sparse vegetation of their winter range.

Mountain lion researchers generally consider it a misconception that the lion is responsible for any decline in deer herds. Looking out over the herd of wintering deer, I knew that many would not survive the bitterly cold temperatures in the months ahead—the old, the infirm, the young, the less fit. This age-old process of population management keeps the herds healthy by preventing overgrazing, maintains ecologic stability, and strengthens the gene pool. Reduction in deer herds is more likely attributed to the impact of modern civilization and habitat loss.

It was now daylight. Seeing no sign of a cougar, the hunters doubled back to a high plateau. There, lion tracks were finally spotted. The trail of a "big tom" stretched from the road's edge, up a slight incline and out of sight. Moliter jumped out of the truck and strapped on his .45 caliber Colt while his partner opened the kennels and brought out the bloodhounds. Radio and shock collars were slipped over the heads of the howling dogs and securely fastened. The collar on one of the

Autumn leaves, harbingers of long winter months ahead, are also the inauspicious heralds of the season when humans hunt mountain lions.

Like an African lioness, the cougar trains her young to hunt by quietly studying the prey animal's movement and behavior.

hounds was also equipped with a mercury switch. When a dog tilts his head to look up a tree, the device transmits a signal to a receiver the hunter holds, indicating that a lion has been treed.

With his dogs eagerly sniffing the ground, Moliter followed the tracks, quickly moving away from his client, the pickups, and the film crew. He returned after thirty minutes and kenneled up the hounds. The cougar tracks were lost, eluding both the hunter's eye and the dogs' nose.

Until dusk we followed the hunting outfit over backcountry roads. We descended into narrow, walled gulches where small springs and seeps flow in spring and early summer. Later, barely oozing from the subsurface and tiny crevices in the canyon walls, their collective moisture irrigates willows, aspens, mountain alder, wild potentilla, currants, chokecherries, snowberry, and wild roses—forage or water for the deer, the coyote, and the white-tailed jack rabbit. Now, a chilling silence stilled the air.

As I entered my motel room at the end of the long day, my weary body numb with cold, I reminded myself that tomorrow morning I would rise again at 2:30 A.M. and begin the search once more.

Sleep was no more than a mirage that night. By 4:30 A.M. we were back on the road. By 6:30 the track was hot. Moliter and his partner had spotted a cougar as it ran across the road in pursuit of a deer. Since Idaho law does not permit the release of cougar hounds until sunrise, the hunters had to wait more than an hour to begin their chase. Moliter was wired with energy. He jumped in and out of his truck, outfitted the dogs, smoked cigarettes, and sharply shouted orders at his partner and my crew. "There's no way in hell this cat will get away," he told his client. It was a big tom and his hounds would be fast on its tail.

Once released from their kennels, the howling dogs ran, nose to the ground, in hot pursuit of the mountain lion. Following their route with an antenna and radio receiver, Moliter was annoyed when the dogs circled some rocks and lost the scent. But they picked it up several minutes later and the transmission soon signaled that the cougar was treed.

Moliter was extremely excited. "That cougar's in *bad* trouble! My hounds got him up a tree. He's in bad trouble now. Neil, we're gonna get that cat. We're gonna get him good!"

Burdened with camera and sound equipment, my crew and I followed the hunters a half-mile uphill toward the barking dogs. But before any of us reached the treed cat, it jumped its perch and ran past us, down the hill, across the road and into a deep gully. The cougar was near exhaustion now. As the dogs ran closer, it forced its last effort to climb another tree, a small alder next to a creek. The lion was one hundred yards from the trucks and only ten yards from the road.

Moliter rushed down the hill past me, yelling, "Dutcher, if you wanna get pictures of this cat, you'd better get your ass down there quick. This cat's dead!"

As far as I could figure, I wasn't holding up the show. Moliter's client, who had paid a lot of money to kill this cougar, was fifty yards behind me, breathing hard.

Positioning myself and my movie camera as quickly as possible, I focused on the terrified lion, silhouetted by the dim morning light. I turned the camera as Neil aimed his pistol.

Two shots!

The first shot stung the cat's chest. A second bullet struck the spinal column, paralyzing the hindquarters. The cougar fell fifteen feet to the stream below. It thrashed as blood spurted from its body into the rushing water.

Now Moliter took aim. Two more shots. The bullets' heat smoked in the fatal wound. "That's a damn good cat, Neil. You got yourself a trophy cat."

Over 1,800 majestic mountain lions are shot every year in the western United States by licensed hunters using electronic tracking equipment and dogs. Another one to two hundred are shot by Animal Damage Control, a federal agency.

8

Winter Logistics

Six months had passed since the construction of the cougar enclosure. Autumn was writing its perennial messages at every turn. Four weeks earlier, aspens shimmered and glowed vibrant yellow against blue-sky days, and their cascading leaves carried golden sunlight to the forest floor. Now, in the skeletal stillness of late October, squirrels busily garnered pinecones in tidy caches. We found these miniature storehouses tucked into the crook of a fallen branch or in fist-sized depressions in the ground. Field mice scurried through the cook tent, even in daylight, brash in their need to fatten up for the long winter ahead.

Catrina's three cubs continued to be quite feral. Their release into the wilderness the following spring would be preceded by six months of heavy snowfall that would close off access to the enclosure by four-wheel-drive vehicles. This inaccessibility to the cougars presented numerous concerns about maintaining and feeding them in their remote winter situation. We figured that they could be fed larger quantities of poultry and roadkills, since the meat would stray fresh in the wintery temperatures at seven thousand feet. Leaving more food at one feeding would allow the cougars to be fed every three days. In warmer weather, we worried that another carnivore—bear, coyote, badger, or even a wild cougar—might pick up

Catrina crouches, attempting to conceal herself before a charge.

their scent and try to get into the enclosure. The black bear's long period of hibernation, however, eliminated much of that concern.

I hired Brent Snider and Kathy Rogerson, the cougars' caretakers when we were away from camp, to work through the winter. They lived five miles from the enclosure and, in winter, travelled by snowmobile from their small ranch to the main road where they kept a car. Not only would they bring food to the cougars by snow machine, but they would also be able to transport the film crew and equipment into the site for winter filming sessions.

Winter arrived, shaking its fist at the drought and warmth of the preceding two years. Chilling winds brought subzero temperatures from the arctic north and frequent storms buried the valleys and alpine summits, layer upon layer, with a heavy blanket of snow. The Sawtooth Valley is consistently one of the coldest places in the continental U.S., with the mercury often plummeting to a fierce forty degrees below zero. Brent told me to expect a minimum of five feet of snow and drifts of seven or eight feet.

I thought of Catrina, her kittens, and the piercing cold. Catrina's coat did not appear to get heavier as autumn temperatures steadily dropped. Instead, she looked sleek, and her tawny fur continued to shed as she prepared to replace her summer coat with a denser and darker winter version. Mountain lions are capable of enduring extremes of hot or cold—even long periods of time swimming in cold water—by adjusting their skin surface temperature to the ambient temperature.

My concern for the cougars' welfare and the continuation of the project deepened as the winter's harshness and early snowpack dramatically increased. Normally, after a long drought, I would join the farmers and ranchers in being grateful for so much moisture. However, this winter I could only think about the possibility that one of the cougars might escape. The repercussions were unthinkable. Harm to the cougar or the wintering elk herd were my first fears. I also realized that I

South-facing rock outcroppings radiate warmth even on the coldest of winter days.

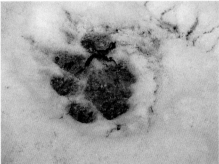

Resplendent blue-sky days ease the harsh temperatures of a long Rocky Mountain winter.

A pawprint melts the winter's first snowfall.

would be liable for any cougar-related mishap within a hundred miles. In addition to the threat of heavy snow buildup, the electric charge in the wiring atop the enclosure fence came from battery packs that were severely weakened by the intense cold and that needed to be changed frequently in the winter months.

These concerns and the desire to film Catrina and her cubs in a winter setting gave us the incentive to make the freezing snowmobile journey into the site ten times that winter. On one typical excursion, we arrived at our rendezvous, and, while waiting for Brent, began piling on various layers of Synchilla, Gortex, and down. When Brent arrived, we applied the final touches—wool hats, goggles, neck-gaiters, and mittens—before loading the snowmobiles and sleds with camera and sound gear, batteries, and a large road-killed buck for Catrina and her cubs.

I stood on the back of the sled like a driver in the Alaskan Iditarod race. However, there were no strong huskies pulling this sled; only a noisy machine interrupting the snow-blanketed stillness of the landscape. I could see the elk herd on a sun-melted south slope, browsing on sparse bushes.

Twenty minutes later, as the snowmobile entourage approached the enclosure, Catrina bounded through the snow to the gate. She paced the fence, waiting anxiously for us to come inside or, more likely, to give her some turkey legs. Her cubs were nowhere in sight.

We set up a blind near the creek. Hiding inside the blind, I readied my camera gear while Jake dragged the deer carcass across the snow and dropped it about forty feet from the blind. He joined me. Catrina had already started gnawing on the deer, even while Jake was trying to bring it into camera position. She plucked the fur for about fifteen minutes, then chirped for her cubs to join her in this unexpected feast.

As always, Casper was the first to appear. He suspiciously made his way down from the rocks across the sunlit snow. He stopped frequently, looking back to the rocks as if to question the wisdom of his decision to investigate what his mother was up to. He looked magnificent! It was February and the cubs were seven months old.

I had not seen any of them this closely for four months. Dashing at the hind-quarter his mother had ripped open, Casper energetically yanked at the leg and shook it in a high-spirited, mischievous show of pride. But, as quickly and proudly as he took possession of the carcass, he froze, as if momentarily caught in an act of villainy, shifted his eyes from left to right, then voraciously resumed his attack.

It was not until ten minutes had passed that Marley and Spook made their way down to the deer. Catrina backed off, leaving the carcass to her offspring who tore into it with a chaotic mix of hunger, competition, and playful gymnastics. Kill sites where lion cubs have eaten are ravaged landscapes scattered with the debris of their jubilance—ears, hide, teeth, and fur. Even in their disorderly manner cubs seem to do a more efficient job of consuming their prey than a solitary adult.

Catrina's three cubs, weighing (I guessed) fifty to fifty-five pounds, were stunning against the stark winter background. Their thick, fluffy fur may have made them look bigger than their true size, but it also indicated their healthy condition. The spots and dark markings had vanished, leaving only faint stripes on their legs like an afterimage.

When they had eaten their fill, Catrina joined them as they wrestled and licked one another clean. Forty feet away, hidden from their view, I filmed the four mountain lions sharing a familial tenderness and affection that has eluded the eye of most humans. They were serene, soft, powerful, alert. Their beauty was heightened by the snow and the low, warm light of the winter sun. The lions were more striking to me in winter than in any other season. Snow simplified the landscape. Now I saw the cougars cleanly without the clutter of surrounding camouflage.

After covering the carcass with snow, the cubs eventually wandered away

With the winter migration of deer from the mountains and onto the prairie, cougars must hunt elk or survive on small prey like the snowshoe hare.

Catrina feasts on a roadkill deer brought into the enclosure by the film crew. Her cubs, now eight months old and quite wild, hide out in the trees to avoid humans.

along paths they had trampled—probably to their den, a snow cave under the big, fallen fir on the far side of the enclosure. Catrina stayed behind and followed us to the gate. She paced and purred as we loaded the sleds and drove away.

As winter warmed into March and we visited the cougars more often, I began to sense relief that, with the worst of winter behind us, the cougars had survived. I remember reflecting one afternoon on this good fortune, when the phone rang. Brent was on the line. A cub was dead! He had found it outside the enclosure—its leg and neck broken and a twelve-inch strip of flesh ripped from its side.

As it was too late in the day to reach the site before dark, I asked Brent to take the cub back to his house to protect it from further ravage and to meet us at the highway rendezvous the following morning. I called Maurice Hornocker, who flew in from northern Idaho that evening.

When we arrived at the enclosure the next day, Brent, carrying the dead cub over his shoulders, led us to a patch of bare earth under a fir tree. He placed the poor cougar on the ground, in the position in which he had discovered it. Instantly I recognized it as Marley. Maurice gently inspected the animal's wounds, then told me the cub had been killed by another cougar. A wild cougar.

We circled the enclosure as Maurice pointed out various signs that sharpened the disastrous picture. Large lion paw prints were visible in the snow a few feet from the dead cub. Along the fence, blood and tufts of fur in a shallow depression revealed where the cub had been killed. On the hillside, inside the fence, we saw streaks through the snow where Catrina must have dashed down to the cries of her young cub.

Catrina, on the other side of the fence, walked along with us. She seemed uneasy. Her two cubs were hidden. Brent told us that he had spent two hours the previous day inspecting the area, and the cubs stayed high up in a tree the entire time. We followed tracks around the north fence line until we found the spot where the cub must have landed as he escaped the enclosure. The snowdrift inside was five feet deep; well-packed and half the height of the fence. Evidently the cat, curious about something outside the fence, sprang from the drift to a precarious balance on a horizontal piece of wood that supported the electric wire. From there he leapt over the top to an aspen branch. Once outside, the cub, not comprehending how to return to its mother, made enough noise to attract the wild lion, within whose territory the enclosure had been built.

Hornocker's extensive research into the mountain lion's behavioral patterns reveals that the animal is extremely dependent on its territorial system to limit population density. Because the cougar sits at the top of the food chain, its species cannot afford the indefinite increases in population that would threaten the prey base. Therefore, a social system and territorial marking define what Hornocker calls "mutual avoidance," or the lion's "land tenure system," the means by which cougars self-regulate their numbers and organize spatial distribution.

A resident cougar—one that has maintained attachment to an area for six months or more—delineates its home range by scratching together twigs, pine needles, dirt, and leaves into piles measuring 5"–15" long, 5"–10" wide, and 1"–2" deep, upon which the lion urinates or defecates to leave a scent. Additional scenting is made by various glands that announce reproductive and residential status. For maximum impact, scrapes are deliberately formed in conspicuous groupings of one to six per site, just off the trail, on high ridges or lion crossings—most often where the topography offers easy passage.

The scrapes serve as olfactory as well as visual warnings to a potential intruder or a transient cougar—usually a young lion seeking to establish its own territory. Coming upon a scrape, the interloper will veer off in a different direction to avoid conflict. The cougar is a solitary animal and relies for survival on its individual physical well-being and strength rather than the communal hunting skill of a pack.

Winter travel is restricted by deep snow, and the mountain lion's territory may dwindle to twenty square miles. The animals frequent sun-melted south slopes where they are likely to find prey.

The eight-
month-old
Casper gives
the crew
a rare,
beautiful,
and rewarding
glimpse.

After a heavy snowstorm in
late March, the cub, Marley,
escaped the enclosure and
was killed by a wild mountain lion defending his
territory.

Therefore, a cougar will avoid a fight to protect its territory. However, if its scrapes are ignored, a resident lion may attack and kill a trespasser. This is apparently what befell our cub, although in rather unusual circumstances.

These demarcations, made frequently by male lions and rarely by females, are seldom found within the core of the range but are scratched in rigid boundaries or in areas that might overlap another cougar's territory. It appears that males never associate with one another and, although their boundaries may be adjacent, they never overlap. Any travel into an adjacent male territory is exploratory and brief.

But a male's range does overlap with the territories of the females with whom he will breed. It is also believed that female territories intersect one another to enhance hunting success. Deer and elk respond to the presence of lions by moving away. Because a female with young demands more prey and the full use of her range is restricted by the mobility of her kittens, her presence and the presence of neighboring females keeps the ungulate herd moving between lion ranges.

Territorial boundaries are flexible. The seasonal movement of prey and deep winter snows may change boundaries or restrict a lion from the higher elevations of its range. The death of a resident leaves scrapes unattended, allowing expansion of an adjacent range. Researchers now understand that human activity such as logging, road building, and excessive hunting might stress lions, causing them to act unexpectedly and more aggressively in defense of their territory. The primary evidence includes increased numbers of scrapes and killing of intruding lions.

▾ ▾ ▾

For many wintery months the female mountain lion has been successful in locating and capturing elk, enough to keep herself and, more importantly, her two fast-growing cubs satisfied. Even so, they continued to nurse sporadically until four months ago. Their mother's swollen teats have receded, leaving behind a slackness of skin and fur that now sways slightly as she walks along.

She is leading her cubs, a male and a female, to the western reaches of her territory, farther down the river drainage, where the elk herds have travelled to escape unusually heavy March snows. This is the most adventurous journey the almost ten-month-old cubs have made, but they are capable, as their mother has moved them progressively farther distances from the different dens to her kill sites since they were quite young.

Now they walk behind her. The silver-coated female leads her darker, fawn-colored brother. He follows her tracks, as she follows their mother who breaks trail. Each lion is unconsciously precise about the placement of its paws, and with each step a hind foot descends perfectly into the snow-molded forepaw track. Their shadowstepping conserves energy, but it is also an extremely useful skill in silently approaching prey. They travel on across an exposed stretch of snow-covered talus slope—lithe, gray shapes diffused in the faint light of early dawn. The female lion senses a security in these early hours.

The day's first light shimmers on the high peaks and is woven into the folds of low clouds. The female and her young soon come to a narrow ledge that overlooks a deep ravine and the heavily wooded lower slopes she has been seeking. A year ago she hunted elk in this drainage. She is also near the territory of her mate; his territory begins just beyond the next ridge. An encounter with him this year will be avoided for the protection of her two young cubs. The clouds plunge lower, suffocating the precipitous landscape in a languorous vapor. Looking between the particles of moisture to the scenery beyond, the female cougar is drawn contentedly into the familiarity of her domain. Her cubs rest calmly by her side, but only for moments. She rouses them with repeated chirps. They follow her descent to the distant watercourse and the elk herd she knows to be near.

The remaining two cubs, Casper and Spook, hide high in a Douglas fir as Dutcher and Dr. Hornocker inspect the circumstances of the cub's death.

9

Leaving Home

By the second week in May the snow on the road to the enclosure had melted away. Warm chinook breezes evaporated the moisture enough to allow us to maneuver our four-wheel-drive vehicles over muddy tracks. We made several trips up to the camp that week to carry in the tents, cabinets, kitchen gear, and all the other equipment necessary to start up the film operation. The thought that I again had access to Catrina, Spook, and Casper lifted many of my fears about the animals' safety. The unfortunate loss of Marley had been constantly on my mind.

A month from now we would release the two lion cubs into the wild, hoping that their destinies would be more fortunate than their brother's. At eleven months old they would be only a month younger than cubs at their earliest natural separation age. Between the ages of twelve and twenty months lion cubs begin a search for a permanent residence away from their maternal territory. Their dispersal, which might take them as far as two hundred miles away, is essential to avoid inbreeding. The circumstances of the Florida Panther, where insufficient habitat eliminates dispersal, create a worst-case scenario for the prospects of genetic diversity.

Several factors may determine when the cubs separate from their mother. Because there is such a diversity in ages of separation between different popula-

Surrounded by the textures of sage and dappled granite, a tranquil cub gazes through late spring snowflakes.

tions of mountain lions, it is assumed that local and regional influences determine the time of separation. Some researchers suggest, for example, that the mother encourages the young ones to leave when their appetites place too heavy a demand on the availability of prey. Her territory becomes too small. In a sort of mutual agreement, the cubs wander increasingly farther distances from their mother for longer periods as they gain independence through hunting proficiency. They return to her side until one excursion takes them away for good. Others believe that the mother leaves her cubs at a kill site, as she has done all their lives when she travels on to hunt for more prey. Except that this time she does not return. It is also possible that her hormones will begin to change and her scent attract a male lion whose presence is enough to send the cubs packing.

Even though Spook and Casper would be younger than most cubs leaving their mother, there is evidence that orphaned cubs as young as five or six months can survive if there is an adequate amount of small prey. Hornocker found that orphaned kittens, raised and fed in secluded captivity until six or seven months old, can be successfully reintroduced to the wild if the manner of feeding not only prevents attachment to humans, but also makes human contact a negative experience. Small mammals—ground squirrels, mice, and chipmunks—are introduced. In this scenario researchers also attempt to parallel the process by which the mother lion associates her cubs' instinct to kill with their choice of appropriate prey so they will learn to selectively pursue animals as food. If captive cubs raised without a mother from whom they can learn survival skills are capable of independence, our cubs had an advantage—Catrina had taught them well.

During their last month of confinement the cubs needed as much hunting practice as possible. We would have to devise a means of feeding them small rodents without their knowing the source. The supply for these lessons would be

A cougar cub assumes a
meditative pose common
to all felines.

Casper prepares for leaving the security of maternal care by catching his own prey.

the ubiquitous ground squirrel. These buffy gray "diggers" inhabit meadows, sagebrush prairie, and agricultural land. Appearing active during the hottest hours of the day, the little critters busy themselves by burrowing extensive tunnels and holes in the ground. Their holes and churned-up earth help control runoff, but their ravenous eating habits can destroy crops. As a favorite small prey of mountain lions, their availability keeps lions quite busy on hot days that would otherwise restrict activity.

They were also a perfect hunting tutorial for Catrina's cubs. Jake rigged a cage for the squirrels. After placing one or two inside, he set the box on the ground in the enclosure. A long cord was tied to the top of the box and stretched over tree limbs and down to a blind where we waited until one or both of the cubs came close. At that moment, Jake pulled the rope which lifted the cage. The squirrels were free to run.

The scenario was often a comedy of errors as the cubs tried to catch a squirrel. As soon as the lid was lifted, the squirrels darted in different directions away from the bewildered cubs. Casper would pounce, misjudging his aim, and pounce again just as the squirrel darted off in another direction. Spook was more reticent, but he may have been more successful because the prey that Casper missed frequently ended up in his mouth. Sometimes a tenacious little squirrel would jump up and bite an unsuspecting cub on the nose. Such bravado in the face of certain doom usually gave the animal another chance, if not escape.

As the cubs got more practice, they became quite adept at capturing their prey. They would have little trouble in the wild, where there would be an ample supply of small animals upon which to hone their skills before attempting more substantial prey. Once freed, they would likely linger together for about a week.

Catrina, the constant tutor, wrestles a cub to the ground.

An affectionate mother bids
farewell to her youngster the
day before the Spook and
Casper are released into the
wild.

Taking a break from the tedium
of a film session, a cub climbs
its favorite tree. Cougars are
possibly the best climbers of
all cats.

During that time they would share their kills, but their lives as social creatures
would come to an end as they left one another to begin the search for a territory.

That journey might keep a young transient, floater, or interloper wandering until it is three or four years old. Conversely, a newly independent female cougar might just walk right into an abandoned range near its area of birth. Scientists do not know the specific mechanism for territorial selection, but they speculate that population density is the most significant factor. This is why the removal of lions through hunting or predator control programs is now considered to be ineffective. Removal might actually increase density while two or more transients compete for the vacant territory. Not only can control attempts be futile, but increased density might cause the transient lions, who are more opportunistic than established residents, to find inadequate territories in fragmented habitat. Here the pressures of insufficient natural prey can increase chances of depredation and even attacks on humans as the cougar moves closer to impinging civilization.

The threat posed by proximity to human activity was the predominant influence in our decision to release Spook and Casper in an extremely remote location that Hornocker felt had the least hunting pressure. We knew that the cubs had an established fear of humans, a fear that is normal in lions. So we felt assured that they would keep their distance. Catrina, as a cougar positively conditioned to humans, would be easy prey for the hunter's gun or she might playfully attack someone who could panic. She might then cause a serious injury.

Her increasingly erratic behavior was testimony to these fears. She stalked the crew more frequently and responded less submissively to our shouts of "No!" when she tried to jump on one of us. There were two most likely reasons for Catrina's aggressive behavior. She had become accustomed to playing roughly with her cubs. These feline games of ambush and attack are the mother cougar's way of teaching her cubs to be alert and competent hunters. A trainer in a zoo would have taken a mother's cubs to a different pen at an earlier age, so there are no records of separation in captivity. Yet Hornocker believed Catrina was naturally preparing to be rid of her cubs and her moods reflected an annoyance at the number of animals in a small space.

Regardless of the reasons for Catrina's dangerous behavior, she continued to attack at unexpected times. The most serious attack was on my second cameraman, Franz Camenzind, just two evenings before we released the cubs. We had closed Catrina in the small pen during a filming session so we could work without worrying about her antics. After completing our work, Jake released her. She dashed down to the pond, then back up the hill, stopping suddenly by my side. After batting her paw at me and curiously gnawing on Franz' leg, she raced away. I knew she was acting up and told everyone to cautiously head for the gate. Franz backed about ten yards off the trail, positioning himself downhill to film if she charged us. Catrina's view of him must have been fragmented by bushes or the angle of the sun. Sparked by his motion, she raced toward Franz and sprang through the air, knocking him and the Arriflex to the ground. She grasped his neck and head in her jaws and wrapped her forelegs around his torso. I ran to Franz, booted Catrina once, and she backed off. She had lanced Franz' skull with a sharp-pointed canine tooth and ripped his ear. His body was covered with claw marks. Catrina's attack was triggered by Franz' distance from the rest of the crew and his quick movements that she was unable to decipher. She certainly had no fear of him nor any of us as a wild cougar would. Any large predator raised in daily contact with humans would be at jeopardy in the wild. Set free, the animal might approach a human for food or linger too long in a hunter's gun sight and be shot. Catrina's freedom would never extend any farther than the five-acre enclosure she now inhabited.

In mid-June, at the age of eleven months, Casper hisses and snarls a warning to stay away. Because these cubs exhibited a fear of humans from six weeks of age, it was decided to release them into the wild upon maturity.

Dutcher and Hornocker carry a cub tranquilized for the move. At eleven months old, each cub weighs one hundred pounds, or two-thirds its adult weight.

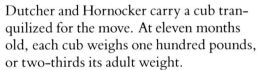

The cubs are transported to a remote area of the 2.3-million-acre Frank Church River of No Return Wilderness in central Idaho.

Her cubs, however, were only a day away from experiencing an expanse of space limited only by the territorial restrictions common to wild mountain lions.

The evening following Catrina's attack on Franz, we prepared to tranquilize the cubs so they could be taken out of the enclosure. Maurice Hornocker carefully measured out a specific amount of drug for his rifle-fired syringe dart and the film crew loaded their packs with gear. Maurice and I entered the enclosure and, after securing Catrina in the small pen, we began to search for her cubs. We found them in the brushy undergrowth near their den. Motionless, they stared and waited for us to walk on as we usually did to minimize contact. As Maurice raised his dart gun and aimed at Casper, the cub ran off, but not fast enough. The dart hit him in the rump as he disappeared over the hill. Spook vanished as quickly. While Maurice pursued him, I followed Casper's trail and discovered him five minutes later in the Aspen grove by the creek. The drug had taken effect and Casper lay on the ground, immobile and glassy-eyed. Maurice soon found Spook and tranquilized him.

Even in their drugged condition the cubs were difficult to manage. They were bigger than Catrina now. Lifting their cumbersome bodies over the creek and through the marsh to the far gates was a difficult task. We chose these gates to avoid carrying the cubs past Catrina in her pen. Once we had them outside, Maurice examined their teeth, claws, and ears and confirmed their sex as masculine. As he finished measuring Spook's tail and body length, the cub started coming to. Casper was already a bit too alert for our comfort. So we loaded them into crates in the back of a pickup and drove them up the road, out of the range of Catrina's hearing.

The following morning we transported the cubs to the Stanley airstrip and flew them by backcountry plane and then by helicopter to a remote wilderness site. We unloaded the sturdy aluminum cages from the helicopter and lifted the doors for the cubs' escape. Neither of them would budge. There was no way they were anxious to come out after all they had been through. Finally we tilted the cages up on end and the cubs scooted out, snarling. They trotted away into the unfamiliar landscape, across a creek, through a stand of pines, and out of sight.

Although released simultaneously, Casper and Spook would most likely hunt together for a week and then travel their separate ways in search of their own territory and a solitary existence.

10

The Ghost Unveiled

If all the beasts were gone, men would die from a great loneliness of spirit, for what happens to the beasts also happens to man. All things are connected. Whatever befalls the earth befalls the sons of the earth. —CHIEF SEATTLE

After Spook and Casper were taken from their mother, Catrina chirped incessantly throughout the night. She wandered the borders of her enclosure with unavailing determination to find her young. Her rueful lamentations penetrated the canyon silence and echoed off the high cliff wall. As the long night wore on, I imagined desperation in her cries. They became louder; coarse and shrill. It might have been impatience I sensed, not desperation. I thought I might be transferring my own emotions into Catrina's wails—a sadness that my time with the cougars was drawing to a close. And yet, why would she not mourn the loss of her cubs or be confused by their disappearance? She cried out this way when Marley was killed. Now she cried for two days. Then quiet returned to our canyon.

Maurice Hornocker, writing about the mountain lion, said he was certain in all his years of research that lions had spent many more hours observing his behavior than he had theirs. It is this cryptic nature that is paradoxically the hole in the cougar's armor and its salvation. For centuries the animal's reality remained shrouded behind veiled truths; its mystery enlivened a spirit of imagination, albeit

As the warm hues of autumn surround the camp and the film project comes to an end, Dutcher and the crew prepare to part with Catrina.

Hindsight tells us that many animals are listed as endangered only after their numbers have dwindled below species survival. No one can say how many cougars live today, but we do know that human encroachment on their habitat is growing dramatically.

baneful. The very fears of the unknown, the legends and myths that once condemned the animal to extinction, surprisingly begin to offer it protection late in the twentieth century. The mystery and the unexplainable again kindle our imagination. Not to banish our fears, but to discover how the cougar and humankind, in our separate realities, are integral to a system that sustains us both.

We see conflicting pictures of the mountain lion through the eyes of hunters, ranchers, scientists, wildlife managers, and preservationists. Each viewpoint, like a piece of glass in a kaleidoscope, is a shard, a fragment until it is combined with the other pieces to create a total image. A slice of the kaleidoscopic pie reveals a jumbled scenario. Ranchers dislike cougars, convinced they are an economic liability. Researchers know that the elimination of cougars by predator control agencies tends to increase rather than reduce the problems of depredation. The programs themselves are drastically more expensive in taxpayer dollars than are the monetary losses to the rancher. Hunters justify killing cougars with the idea that they prey upon too many of the deer that the hunters want to kill. In reality deer numbers suffer not from cougar predation but from competition by livestock, poaching, and roadkills. A licensed hunter kills a cougar for sport, for the trophy. Hunting license fees fund the departments that manage the wildlife that is killed. These funds also help department researchers study the lion to protect it from overharvesting. However, it is a myth that harvest figures are an accurate means of determining actual numbers of cougars alive or dead. Overharvesting, along with increasing incidences of poaching, could threaten the stability of mountain lion populations, which in turn triggers the concern of preservationists. Their ultimate goal is to protect the cougar and the wild lands that serve as its sanctuary. Amidst all of the confusion there is one point of accord: The cougar is headed straight for serious ecological danger unless the special interest groups join minds in decisions concerning the animal's future.

The cougar's exhilaration, grace, and mystery serve as a symbol for the wildness and freedom that nurture the human spirit.

With the wolf and grizzly endangered in the United States, the cougar has settled into the status of dominant predator.

Catrina is taken from the enclosure to her new home on a crisp autumn day, and Dutcher's cougar project draws to a close.

At present the mountain lion is not threatened in the western United States. But it is only a romantic illusion that all is well; that the vastness of mountain spaces offers America's lion an idyllic asylum from the pursuits of humans. There are many unanswered questions about the mountain lion's behavior, ecology, and biology. Ironically, the lion's mechanism for survival—elusion—makes it the most difficult of all large predators to locate and study. Scientists are concerned that decisions about the lion and its habitat are being made without sufficient knowledge of the species. Among the most urgent concerns are the effects of hunting on specific lion populations. Most states have only an educated guess as to the number of cougars roaming their mountains and prairies. This fact alone necessitates a refinement of hunting regulations and more efficient techniques to monitor and quantitate populations. Researchers need to know more about the territorial requirements and social structure of lions living in fragmented habitat as well as wilderness. Congress needs to designate new wilderness areas. Buffer zones for wildlife need to be created around national parks. States need to promote the lion as a valuable aesthetic resource. The mountain lion needs to become an image in the eye of public awareness.

Clearly, the extensive hatred of the cougar lives in the past. And killing as a symbolic act of heroism is defunct. Barraged with the potential consequences of perpetuating past indignities to our animals and environment, civilization is creating new symbols: wilderness as sanctuary. Wildlife as the mirror of our own well-being.

The survival of the cougar is dependent upon personal connection; a sense of awe and reverence, an intimate knowledge. Catrina offered me this affinity. Some say that my approach to making a film about the mountain lion was irreverent; that I broke the traditional rules of natural history filmmaking. I ask if it is more important to honor the rigors of tradition than to unveil mystery; to ignore rather than to illuminate the clandestine nature of America's lion. Unfortunately, it is too late for humankind to leave the cougar alone. If the cougar is to retain its presence in the wilds; if it is to be more than a relic of America's heritage, then Americans need to merge their spirits with the spirit of the cougar.

Late in September I said my farewell to Catrina. She was to be taken from the Boise Zoo to her permanent home at the Olympic Game Farm. I left her in the same back-lot pen where I had found her a year and a half earlier. Leaning against the cage, I spoke her name softly over and over. I wanted her attention; an assurance that I had meant something to her, as she had to me. Instead, crouched on a high bench, head thrust forward, she fixed her eyes on a woolly bison as it walked up to her cage to rub its enormous face on the fencing. With the bison so near, she seemed drawn away by a silver thread of memory into the wild places of her mind. And I was invisible. I walked away. But I turned back to see her one last time. Now her eyes caught mine. I could not help but imagine a kinship, an emotional exchange between two different creatures briefly travelling together. I hovered for seconds in Catrina's eyes, then she resumed her vigil over the bison.

"Any glimpse into the life of an animal quickens our own and makes it so much larger and better in every way."—JOHN MUIR

About the Authors

KAREN McCALL

Author Karen McCall has worked on nuclear and environmental issues in the Northwest for the past fifteen years. For two years she lived in Idaho's backcountry working as researcher and production assistant for Jim Dutcher's film *Cougar: Ghost of the Rockies.* She and Dutcher currently divide their time between their home in Ketchum, Idaho, and a camp in the mountains where they are raising a captive pack of wolves for Dutcher's new film, *Wolf: The Return of a Legend.*

JIM DUTCHER

Producer, director, and cinematographer Jim Dutcher has been documenting wildlife around the globe for thirty years. He began photographing life underwater at fourteen and using a movie camera at seventeen. For the past fifteen years he has lived in Idaho, where his photography and films have concentrated on the natural history of the Rocky Mountains. His films *Water, Birth, the Planet Earth,* a PBS special, and *A Beaver Pond,* for the National Geographic Society have won numerous awards. *Cougar: Ghost of the Rockies* first aired on ABC in 1990 to an audience of twenty million and has since been televised worldwide. Dutcher has received six national and international awards for *Cougar,* including best documentary from the Fund for Animals' Genesis Awards and best factual narrative from the National Cowboy Hall of Fame. Because Dutcher believes that intimacy with his subject is an effective way to develop the widespread human understanding necessary for a species' survival, he often chooses projects that involve animal / human contact.

References

Anderson, A. E. 1983. *A critical review of literature on Puma (Felis concolor)*. Colorado Division of Wildlife. Denver, CO.

Ashman, D. L. and others. 1983. *The mountain lion in Nevada*. Final report for the Nevada Department of Wildlife. Elko, NV.

Barber, E. A. 1876. Rock inscriptions of the "ancient pueblos" of Colorado, Utah, New Mexico, and Arizona. *American Naturalist* 10: 716–725.

Dixon, K. R., and R. J. Boyd. 1967. *Evaluation of the effects of mountain lion predation*. Job completion report for the Colorado Game, Fish and Parks Department.

Dobie, J. F. 1943. Tales of the Panther. *Saturday Evening Post,* Dec. 11, 55–61.

Flowers, C. 1989. Searching for the one true cat. *National Wildlife* 27 (6): 24–28.

Frome, M. 1979. Panthers wanted—alive, back east where they belong. *Smithsonian* 10(3): 83–88.

Grubb, B. G. 1985. The mysterious and misunderstood mountain lion. *Idaho the University* 3 (November): 10–15.

Hornocker, M. G. 1969. Stalking the mountain lion—to save him. *National Geographic* 136 (November): 638–655.

Hornocker, M. G. 1969. The wild and scenic rivers act: how it will affect wildlife and recreation in the northwest. Presented at the first annual winter meeting of the Idaho Chapter Wildlife Society. Boise, ID.

Hornocker, M. G. 1969. Winter territoriality in mountain lions. *Journal of Wildlife Management* 33:457–464.

Hornocker, M. G. 1970. An analysis of mountain lion predation upon mule deer and elk in the Idaho Primitive Area. Wildlife Monographs no. 21.

Hornocker, M. G. 1971. Suggestions for the management of mountain lions as a trophy species in the intermountain region. Paper presented at the Proceedings of the Western Association of State Game and Fish Commissioners. 51:399–402. Snowmass, CO.

Hornocker, M. G. 1978. Interactions between threatened and endangered species and wilderness. Presented at the forty-third American Wildlife Conference of the Wildlife Management Institute. March. Phoenix, AZ.

Johnson, S. 1989. Federal agents killed about 250,000 predators in 1987. *High Country News* 21 (September): 14–15.

Logan, K. A. 1983. *Mountain lion population and habitat characteristics in the Big Horn Mountains of Wyoming*. Master's Thesis for the Wyoming Cooperative Fishery and Wildlife Research Unit. Univ. of Montana, Missoula.

Lopez, B. H. 1978. *Of wolves and men*. New York: Charles Scribner's Sons.

McNamee, T. 1981. Chasing a ghost. *Audubon* (March): 31–35.

Matthiessen, P. 1959. *Wildlife in America*. New York: Viking Penguin.

Morris, C. 1985. Maritime panthers not mythical residents. *Ottawa Citizen,* July 6, E12.

Murphy, K. 1983. *Characteristics of a hunted population of mountain lions in western Montana*. Unpublished thesis ms. Univ. of Montana, Missoula.

146

National Wildlife Federation. 1987. *The kingdom of cats.* Washington, D.C.

Roberson, J., and F. Lindzey, eds. 1984. Proceedings of the second Mountain Lion Workshop. Utah Division of Wildlife Resources. November. Zion National Park, UT.

Satchell, M., and J. M. Schrof. 1990. The American hunter under fire. *U.S. News and World Report,* 5 February, 30–37.

Seidensticker, J. C., and others. 1973. Mountain lion social organization in the Idaho Primitive Area. Wildlife Monographs, no. 35.

Shaw, H. G. 1989. *Soul among lions.* Boulder, CO.: Johnson Books.

Sitton, L. W., and R. A. Weaver. 1977. *California mountain lion investigations with recommendations for management.* Study for the California Department of Fish and Game. Sacramento, CA.

Springer, K. 1987. Looking at the American mountain lion. *Biologue* 2 (Fall): 1–15.

Tinsley, J. B. 1987. *The puma, legendary lion of the Americas.* El Paso, TX.: Texas Western Press.

Trulio, L. 1989. *Mountain lions and depredation.* Pamphlet for the Mountain Lion Foundation. Sacramento, CA

Turbak, G. 1982. The cougar's new cloak. *National Wildlife,* Apr.–May, 47–54.

Turbak, G. 1985. Myth buster. *National Wildlife,* Aug.–Sept., 38–43.

Van Dyke, F. G. and others. 1986. Reactions of mountain lions to logging and human activity. *Journal of Wildlife Management* 50(1):95–102.

Weddle, F. 1966. The cougar: prince of wilderness country. *Defenders of Wildlife News* (Apr.–June) 180–191.

Wilkenson, T. 1989. Driving wild things to extinction. *High Country News* 21 (18 December).

Wilson, P. 1984. Puma predation on guanocos in Torres del Paine National Park, Chile. *Mammalia* 4:515–522.

Wright, B. S. 1959. *The ghost of North America.* New York: Vantage.

Wright, B. S. 1972. *The eastern panther.* Toronto / Vancouver: Clarke, Irwin and Company.

Young, S. P., and E. A. Goldman. 1946. *The puma: mysterious American cat.* New York: Dover Publications.